Whispers of Samhain

Whispers of Samhain

Matthew Petchinsky

1

Halloween is a Powerful time

Whispers of Samhain: 1,000 Spells of Love, Luck, and Lunar Magic: Samhain Spell Book

By: Matthew Petchinsky

Introduction to Samhain: The History, Significance, and Traditions of Samhain

Samhain (pronounced "sow-in") is one of the most important and magical festivals in the pagan calendar, marking a time of transition, reflection, and powerful spiritual energy. Celebrated on October 31st, it originates from ancient Celtic traditions and heralds the end of the harvest season while ushering in the dark half of the year. This festival is steeped in history, filled with rich cultural practices, and revered for its potent spiritual significance. The lore, customs, and magic of Samhain have endured for centuries, evolving into what many now recognize as Halloween.

The History of Samhain

Samhain dates back over 2,000 years to the ancient Celts, who inhabited the regions now known as Ireland, the United Kingdom, and northern France. For the Celts, the year was divided into two main seasons: the light (spring and summer) and the dark (autumn and winter). Samhain marked the end of the light season, the conclusion of the harvest, and the beginning of the dark half of the year. This turning point was seen as the death of the old year and the birth of the new, a period of liminality where the veil between the physical world and the spirit world was at its thinnest.

The ancient Celts believed that during this liminal period, the boundaries between the world of the living and the realm of the dead were blurred. Spirits of ancestors and supernatural beings could cross into the physical world more freely. This made Samhain a time not only to honor deceased loved ones but also to prepare for the challenges of winter. The festival was marked by communal feasts, bonfires, and various rituals to communicate with and honor the spirits, seek guidance, and ward off malevolent entities.

As Christianity spread across Europe, many Samhain customs were adapted into All Saints' Day (November 1st) and All Souls' Day (November 2nd). The evening before these days, known as All Hallows' Eve, eventually evolved into the modern Halloween. Despite the efforts to Christianize the festival, many Samhain traditions persisted, retaining their mystical and magical essence.

The Significance of Samhain

Samhain holds profound significance as a time of death, rebirth, and transformation. It represents the cycle of life—the harvest has ended, the days grow shorter, and nature enters a period of dormancy. Just as the Earth undergoes a natural cycle of death and renewal, Samhain encourages introspection and the release of what no longer serves us. It is a time to let go of the old year's burdens and plant the seeds for new beginnings.

In the spiritual realm, Samhain is a time when the veil between worlds is at its thinnest, allowing for a stronger connection with the otherworldly. This unique period makes it ideal for divination, communication with ancestors, and spellwork. Practitioners often seek guidance for the upcoming year, invite messages from their ancestors, and use the energy of Samhain to perform spells that align with themes of transformation, protection, and new beginnings.

Samhain is also a festival of the ancestors, a time to honor and connect with those who have passed on. This connection can be comforting and healing, as it reminds us of the continuity of life and death. By honoring our ancestors and acknowledging the cycle of life, we gain strength and wisdom to navigate the challenges of the coming winter.

Traditions of Samhain

The traditions of Samhain are numerous and varied, often combining elements of celebration, reverence, and magic. Here are some of the key customs and practices associated with this mystical festival:

1. **Bonfires:** One of the most iconic Samhain traditions involves lighting large communal bonfires. In ancient times, these fires symbolized the sun's power and were believed to ward off evil spirits. People would extinguish their home hearths and relight them from the communal Samhain bonfire, symbolizing unity and the shared strength of the community. Today, bonfires remain a popular way to celebrate, providing warmth and light during the darkening days.

2. **Feasting and Offerings:** Samhain is a time of feasting, both as a celebration of the final harvest and a ritual offering to the spirits and ancestors. Traditional foods include apples, nuts, root vegetables, grains, and meats. During feasts, it was customary to set aside a portion of food and drink as an offering to the spirits. Some modern practitioners set a "dumb supper,"

a silent meal in which a place is set at the table for deceased loved ones, inviting them to join in the festivities.

3. **Divination:** The thinning of the veil between worlds makes Samhain an ideal time for divination. In ancient times, various methods such as scrying, casting runes, and reading tarot cards were used to gain insight into the future. Apples, a symbol of Samhain, were also used in divination practices. One common tradition involved peeling an apple in a single long strip, tossing the peel over the shoulder, and interpreting the shape it formed to reveal the initials of a future lover.

4. **Carving Jack-o'-Lanterns:** The practice of carving turnips or pumpkins into lanterns stems from the Samhain tradition of warding off malevolent spirits. The lanterns were often carved with faces to represent spirits and placed on doorsteps or in windows to protect homes. The modern Jack-o'-lantern, carved from pumpkins and lit with candles, continues this tradition, serving both as decoration and as a magical tool for protection.

5. **Costumes and Disguises:** During Samhain, people would wear costumes and masks to disguise themselves from roaming spirits. The idea was to blend in with the supernatural entities to avoid their attention or wrath. Today, this practice has evolved into the Halloween tradition of dressing up in various costumes, but it still echoes the ancient belief in the thin veil and the presence of spirits.

6. **Honoring the Ancestors:** Remembering and honoring ancestors is a central aspect of Samhain. Altars are often adorned with photos, mementos, and offerings for deceased loved ones. Some people light candles in honor of their ancestors, while others may perform rituals or say prayers to invite the spirits of their ancestors into their homes for guidance and protection. This practice not only honors those who have passed but also strengthens the bond between the living and the spiritual realm.

7. **Magic and Spellwork:** With the veil between worlds being at its thinnest, Samhain is considered one of the most potent times for spellwork and magical practices. Spells cast during this time are said to be particularly powerful, making it an ideal period for performing rituals related to love, luck, protection, transformation, and divination. The energy of Samhain supports the release of negative patterns, the setting of new intentions, and the manifestation of desires for the coming year.

Samhain's Enduring Magic

The magic of Samhain has endured for centuries, evolving with time yet maintaining its mystical core. Modern celebrations of Samhain may vary, but they continue to revolve around the themes of death, rebirth, introspection, and connection with the spiritual world. Whether through quiet reflection, honoring ancestors, casting spells, or simply enjoying the festive atmosphere of Halloween, Samhain offers a powerful opportunity to connect with the cycles of nature and the mysteries of life and death.

As you journey through this spell book, you will discover a collection of 1,000 spells, each harnessing the unique energy of Samhain. From love spells that draw on the enchantment of the season to luck spells that embrace the bountiful harvest, these rituals invite you to explore the depth of Samhain magic. Whether you are a seasoned practitioner or new to the mystical arts, this collection is designed to guide you through the diverse and profound magic that Samhain offers. Prepare your altar, gather your tools, and open your heart to the whispers of Samhain—where the veil lifts, and magic reigns.

Chapter 1: The Power of Samhain Spells: How Samhain Creates a Unique Energy for Spellcasting

Samhain is a time unlike any other in the magical year, revered for its potent energy and unparalleled spellcasting power. For witches, pagans, and spiritual seekers, Samhain represents the turning of the Wheel of the Year and the threshold between light and dark, life and death. This time is ripe for magic, a period when the veil between the worlds is at its thinnest, allowing for a deeper connection with the spiritual realm. Understanding the unique energy that Samhain brings is key to harnessing its full potential for spellcasting.

In this chapter, we will explore what makes Samhain such a powerful time for spellwork, the specific energies it offers, and how you can align yourself with this sacred energy to enhance your magical practices.

1. Samhain's Liminal Space: The Thin Veil Between Worlds

The most defining characteristic of Samhain is its liminal nature. "Liminal" refers to a threshold or boundary—a space between two states. Samhain is precisely this: it is neither the peak of summer nor the depths of winter but a transitional phase that lies at the boundary between these two extremes. This liminality gives Samhain its magical potency. As the final harvest of the year, it represents both an ending and a beginning, making it a time for reflection, release, and rebirth.

One of the most widely recognized aspects of Samhain is the thinning of the veil between the living world and the realm of spirits. During this time, the boundary that separates the physical world from the spiritual realm becomes almost nonexistent. This thinning allows us to communicate more freely with ancestors, spirits, and otherworldly beings, making Samhain an opportune moment for divination, spirit work, and spellcasting.

The thinning of the veil during Samhain also amplifies our intuition and psychic abilities. When you cast spells during this period, your connection to the spiritual world is heightened, allowing your intentions to reach farther and deeper. This connection helps you receive clearer guidance, stronger messages, and more powerful energy to manifest your desires.

2. Samhain's Association with Death and Rebirth

Samhain is often referred to as the "Witch's New Year" because it marks the end of the agricultural year and the beginning of winter. The Celts viewed this time as the death of the old year and the birth of the new. Just as nature enters a phase of dormancy, we are invited to reflect on the cycle of life, death, and rebirth within our own lives. This association with death makes Samhain a powerful time for releasing what no longer serves us—be it negative habits, relationships, or emotional burdens.

Spells performed during Samhain can tap into this cycle of death and rebirth, making it an ideal time for transformative magic. When you cast a spell at Samhain, you are not only setting intentions but also embracing the natural cycle of letting go to make room for new growth. The energy of Samhain encourages you to release the old year's energies, cleanse your aura, and prepare yourself for the possibilities of the new year. This transformative power makes Samhain spells particularly effective for deep, lasting change.

3. Harvest Energies: Abundance and Gratitude

As the final harvest festival, Samhain carries the energies of abundance and completion. It is a time to take stock of what you have gathered throughout the year, both physically and spiritually. The harvest energy of Samhain makes it an excellent time for spells related to prosperity, gratitude, and manifestation.

When you cast spells for abundance or prosperity during Samhain, you are tapping into the natural cycle of the Earth's bounty. By aligning with this harvest energy, your intentions are empowered by the collective gratitude and abundance of nature itself. Spells of gratitude during Samhain can open channels for new opportunities and blessings to flow into your life, as the act of giving thanks creates a fertile ground for further manifestations.

4. The Elemental Forces of Samhain

Samhain's energy is deeply rooted in the natural elements: Earth, Air, Fire, and Water. Each element plays a role in creating the unique spellcasting environment of Samhain:

- **Earth:** With the final harvest and the falling of leaves, the Earth element is strong during Samhain. It represents the cycle of life and death, the grounding energy that supports our magical intentions. Spells focused on grounding, protection, stability, and abundance can draw power from the Earth's energies at this time.
- **Air:** As the crisp autumn winds blow, the Air element brings a sense of change and transformation. It carries the whispers of spirits and the breath of life. Air enhances spells of communication, divination, clarity, and mental focus, making Samhain an ideal time for spellwork that requires guidance, vision, or messages from beyond the veil.
- **Fire:** The tradition of lighting bonfires during Samhain highlights the strength of the Fire element. Fire represents the light within the darkness, the spark of life amidst the cycle of death. It is the perfect element for spells of purification, courage, passion, and transformation. Working with fire during Samhain—whether through candle magic, bonfires, or hearth fires—amplifies your intentions, bringing swift and potent change.
- **Water:** As the rains begin to fall and the days grow shorter, the Water element emerges, symbolizing intuition, emotion, and the flow of life and death. Samhain's water energy is beneficial for spells of healing, cleansing, emotional release, and psychic work. Rituals involving scrying with water, cleansing baths, or libations to spirits tap into the profound depths of Samhain's water energy.

By consciously working with the elemental forces of Samhain, you can enhance your spellcasting and align your intentions with the natural energies of this sacred time.

5. Ancestor Magic: Honoring the Spirits

One of the most significant aspects of Samhain is ancestor veneration. The Celts believed that during Samhain, the spirits of the deceased returned to the mortal realm, allowing the living to commune with their ancestors. This practice is not only an act of remembrance but also a way to gain insight, protection, and guidance from those who have passed on.

Samhain spells often involve ancestor magic, where practitioners call upon the wisdom and energy of their forebears. By connecting with your ancestors, you can draw on their strength and knowledge to support your spellwork. Whether you seek protection, guidance, or a deeper understanding of yourself, your ancestors can offer powerful assistance during Samhain.

Creating an ancestral altar, offering food or drink, lighting candles, and saying prayers are some ways to honor your ancestors and invite their presence into your spellcasting. By integrating ancestor magic into your Samhain spells, you align with the energies of the past and the spiritual world, giving your intentions an added layer of depth and power.

6. Divination and Psychic Enhancement

Due to the thinning of the veil, Samhain is renowned for its enhancement of divinatory practices. This is the perfect time for spells that involve scrying, tarot readings, rune casting, pendulum dowsing, or any form of divination. During Samhain, messages from the spirit world are more accessible, and insights into the future are clearer.

When casting spells for divination, consider using Samhain symbols such as pumpkins, apples, or autumn leaves in your rituals. These elements are imbued with the season's energy and can serve as conduits for spiritual messages. In addition to traditional divination tools, you can create spell jars or charm bags filled with Samhain herbs, crystals, and symbols to enhance your psychic abilities throughout the season.

7. Protection and Banishing Spells

The presence of spirits and supernatural beings during Samhain makes it a time when both positive and negative energies are active. Protection spells cast during Samhain are highly potent because they tap into the protective energy of the season. Using tools like salt, iron, pumpkins, and candles, you can create powerful wards around your home and person.

Samhain is also an ideal time for banishing spells—rituals that remove negativity, toxic relationships, bad habits, or unwanted spirits. The dark, introspective energy of the season supports deep inner work and the release of anything that hinders your growth. The act of banishing during Samhain can be a cathartic process, allowing you to enter the new year free of the past's burdens.

Harnessing Samhain's Unique Energy in Your Spellwork

To make the most of Samhain's energy, it is essential to align your intentions with the themes and natural forces of the season. Here are some ways to harness this unique energy in your spellcasting:

1. **Set Your Intentions:** Before performing any spell, reflect on what you wish to release and what you want to manifest in the new cycle. Write down your intentions to give them a clear focus.

2. **Create a Sacred Space:** Decorate your altar with Samhain symbols like pumpkins, apples, leaves, and candles. Use autumn colors and incorporate elements like bones, skulls, and cauldrons to connect with the energy of the season.

3. **Honor the Spirits:** Light candles for your ancestors, leave offerings, and say prayers to invite their guidance and protection during your spellwork.

4. **Incorporate Elemental Energy:** Use natural elements such as herbs, crystals, water, and fire in your rituals to ground your intentions and draw on the seasonal energies.

5. **Work with Divination:** Begin your spellcasting session with a divination practice to gain insight and direction. This will help you fine-tune your spells and align them with the energies around you.

6. **Be Open to Transformation:** Samhain's energy is about death and rebirth. Be ready to let go of what no longer serves you and embrace new beginnings. Trust that the spells you cast during Samhain will work with this transformative energy to bring about profound change.

Samhain's magic is profound, offering a rare opportunity to connect with the spiritual realm, honor the cycles of life, and manifest your deepest intentions. By understanding and aligning with Samhain's unique energy, you can amplify your spellcasting and bring your desires into reality with the support of this powerful season.

Chapter 2: Preparing for Spellwork: Tools, Ingredients, Altar Setup, and Creating a Sacred Space

Spellwork is an art that requires preparation, intention, and a connection to the natural and spiritual realms. To maximize the power and effectiveness of your Samhain spellcasting, it's essential to carefully prepare your tools, ingredients, altar, and sacred space. This preparation sets the stage for your magical intentions, allowing you to work with focus, purpose, and clarity.

In this chapter, we will explore the essential components for successful spellwork during Samhain, including the tools and ingredients needed, how to set up a spellcasting altar, and the steps to create a sacred space that enhances your magical practices.

1. Essential Tools for Samhain Spellwork

Every practitioner develops their own collection of tools that resonate with their energy and intentions. The tools used for Samhain spellwork are not only practical but also serve as symbols that help direct the flow of energy. Here are some common tools that are especially powerful during Samhain:

- **Athame:** A ritual knife often used to direct energy, cut energetic ties, or carve symbols into candles. During Samhain, the athame can be used to trace protective symbols, draw circles, or carve runes into pumpkins and candles for spellwork.
- **Cauldron:** A symbol of transformation and the cycle of life and death, the cauldron is central to Samhain magic. It can be used to mix herbs, brew potions, burn incense, or hold ritual fires. If you have a small cauldron, use it to burn bay leaves or other herbs to release intentions into the air.
- **Candles:** Candles are a powerful tool for spellwork, representing the element of Fire. For Samhain, use candles in colors that resonate with the season, such as black (protection, banishing), orange (creativity, vitality), and purple (psychic power, divination). Carve symbols or words into the candles before lighting them to focus your intentions.
- **Pentacle:** The pentacle, usually a flat disk inscribed with a five-pointed star, represents the elements of Earth, Air, Fire, Water, and Spirit. Place the pentacle on your altar as a symbol

of protection and balance. It can also serve as a surface for charging objects, crystals, or herbs used in your spellwork.

• **Wand:** Traditionally made from wood, a wand is used to channel and direct energy. During Samhain, consider using wands crafted from seasonal woods such as oak, yew, or apple, which are associated with the magic of the season. Use the wand to trace symbols, draw protective circles, or stir mixtures in your cauldron.

• **Chalice:** A goblet or cup often used to hold ritual liquids, such as water, wine, or herbal brews. The chalice represents the element of Water and the divine feminine. For Samhain, fill the chalice with seasonal drinks like apple cider, mulled wine, or an herbal infusion to honor the spirits and the harvest.

• **Crystals:** Crystals enhance spellwork by adding specific energies. For Samhain, consider using crystals such as obsidian (protection, banishing negativity), amethyst (psychic abilities, spiritual connection), and smoky quartz (grounding, releasing). Place them on your altar or carry them with you during rituals.

• **Incense or Herbs:** Burning incense or herbs can help cleanse your space and raise the vibrational energy for spellwork. Popular choices for Samhain include sage (cleansing), myrrh (spiritual connection), frankincense (protection), and cinnamon (prosperity, warmth). You can burn these herbs or incense during rituals or use them to cleanse your tools and altar.

• **Mortar and Pestle:** This tool is used for grinding herbs and resins. Preparing your own mixtures for spellwork can deepen your connection to the ingredients and the magic of the season. During Samhain, use your mortar and pestle to blend herbs like mugwort, rosemary, and cinnamon for rituals of divination, protection, or abundance.

2. Gathering Ingredients for Samhain Spells

The ingredients used in Samhain spellwork are closely tied to the season, harnessing the natural energies of autumn and the final harvest. Here's a guide to some of the key ingredients you might incorporate into your spells:

- **Herbs:** Seasonal herbs carry the energies of Samhain. Common choices include:
    - **Mugwort:** Enhances psychic abilities and is ideal for divination spells.
    - **Rosemary:** Used for protection and purification, often burned to cleanse spaces.
    - **Sage:** Powerful for cleansing, banishing negativity, and creating sacred spaces.
    - **Cinnamon:** Attracts prosperity, warmth, and positive energy.
    - **Wormwood:** Associated with spirit communication, ideal for rituals connecting with ancestors.
- **Flowers and Plants:** Incorporate autumnal plants such as chrysanthemums (for protection and honoring the dead) and marigolds (for their connection to the spirit world). Dried flowers can be used in charm bags, spell jars, or as offerings on the altar.
- **Fruits and Vegetables:** Seasonal produce like apples, pumpkins, pomegranates, and nuts embody the harvest energy. Apples can be used in love spells or divination rituals, while pumpkins symbolize abundance and can be carved with protective symbols.
- **Oils:** Essential oils are used to anoint candles, tools, and yourself. For Samhain, try oils such as frankincense (spirituality, protection), myrrh (sacred connection), or clove (courage, banishing negativity). Mixing your own oil blends can infuse your spells with personal energy.
- **Salt:** A traditional purifying and protective substance. Use salt to create a protective circle or to cleanse your altar and tools before spellwork.

3. Setting Up Your Samhain Altar

The altar is the focal point of your spellwork, a place where you can gather your tools, ingredients, and symbols to direct your magical intentions. For Samhain, the altar is often decorated to honor the season, the spirits, and the energies of transformation. Here's how to set up a powerful Samhain altar:

1. **Choose a Location:** Select a quiet, undisturbed area for your altar. It could be a small table, shelf, or even a section of the floor. Make sure it is a place where you can focus and work comfortably.

2. **Cover the Altar:** Use an altar cloth in colors that resonate with Samhain, such as black, orange, deep purple, or earthy browns. The cloth not only adds to the atmosphere but also protects the surface of the altar.

3. **Arrange the Tools:** Place your essential tools on the altar. The placement can follow traditional correspondences (e.g., pentacle in the center, candles in the corners, cauldron near the back), or you can arrange them in a way that feels intuitively right for you.

4. **Add Seasonal Symbols:** Decorate the altar with symbols of Samhain, such as small pumpkins, apples, autumn leaves, acorns, and dried flowers. These items infuse the altar with the energy of the season and enhance the power of your spellwork.

5. **Include an Ancestral Corner:** Samhain is a time for honoring ancestors. Dedicate a section of your altar to those who have passed by placing photos, mementos, or a candle to represent their presence. Add offerings like food, drink, or flowers to honor their spirits.

6. **Candles and Incense:** Place candles on the altar to represent the element of Fire. Light them during rituals to focus your energy and set the mood for spellwork. Incense or a smudge stick can be burned to cleanse the space and elevate the vibrational energy.

7. **Charged Objects:** Include any crystals, amulets, or personal objects you want to charge with Samhain energy. Arrange them on the altar, where they can absorb the magical energies of your rituals.

4. Creating a Sacred Space for Samhain Spellwork

Creating a sacred space is a crucial step in preparing for spellwork. It establishes a protective boundary and elevates the energy of the area to support your magical intentions. Here's how to create a sacred space for your Samhain rituals:

1. **Cleanse the Space:** Before beginning any spellwork, cleanse the area to remove any negative or stagnant energy. This can be done by burning sage, cedar, or palo santo, sprinkling salt water around the space, or using a bell or singing bowl to clear the energy with sound.

2. **Cast a Circle:** Casting a circle creates a protected, sacred area for your spellwork. To cast a circle, stand in the center of your space with your athame, wand, or hand extended. Visualize a sphere of light emanating from you, expanding outward to form a circle around your space. Walk clockwise around the area, imagining the light creating a boundary that separates the mundane world from the magical realm.

3. **Call the Quarters:** Many practitioners call upon the elements (Earth, Air, Fire, Water) to aid in their spellwork. As you face each direction, invite the element associated with that direction to join and support your ritual. For example:
   - **East (Air):** "I call upon the element of Air, bringer of insight and clarity. Join this circle and lend your power to my spellwork."
   - **South (Fire):** "I call upon the element of Fire, source of passion and transformation. Join this circle and ignite my intentions."
   - **West (Water):** "I call upon the element of Water, keeper of intuition and emotion. Join this circle and flow through my magic."
   - **North (Earth):** "I call upon the element of Earth, provider of stability and growth. Join this circle and ground my energy."

4. **Set the Intention:** Before beginning any spell, state your intention clearly. This focuses your energy and opens the connection between your inner self and the spiritual forces you are calling upon.

5. **Close the Space:** After completing your spellwork, be sure to close the sacred space by thanking the elements, ancestors, and any spirits you invoked. Walk counterclockwise around the circle, visualizing the boundary dissolving back into the ether.

5. Enhancing the Atmosphere for Samhain Spellwork

To further amplify the energy of your spellwork, consider adding atmospheric elements that resonate with Samhain:

- **Music:** Soft, instrumental music, drumming, or chanting can help you enter a trance-like state and deepen your connection to the spellwork. Choose sounds that evoke the mystery and magic of autumn.
- **Scents:** Use essential oils, incense, or simmering potpourri with scents like cinnamon, clove, frankincense, and patchouli to fill your space with the essence of Samhain.
- **Lighting:** Dimming the lights or working by candlelight adds to the mystical atmosphere. The flickering of candle flames can help you focus and invoke the energies of the fire element.

By carefully preparing your tools, ingredients, altar, and sacred space, you create a powerful environment for your Samhain spellwork. This preparation not only enhances the effectiveness of your spells but also deepens your connection to the magic and spirit of the season. As you work within your sacred space, you align yourself with the energies of Samhain, transforming your intentions into reality with the power of the ancient festival.

Chapter 3: Spellcasting Basics: Essential Knowledge for Beginners, Including Intent, Focus, and Timing

Spellcasting is a practice that requires a balance of knowledge, intention, and mindfulness. While the specific ingredients, tools, and rituals vary, the core principles of magic remain consistent. In this chapter, we will delve into the fundamentals of spellcasting, focusing on the concepts of intent, focus, timing, and other essential practices that every beginner should master. Understanding these basics will not only enhance the effectiveness of your Samhain spells but also empower you to practice magic safely and confidently.

1. Understanding Intent: The Heart of All Magic

Intent is the foundation of all spellwork; it is the driving force behind every magical act. In its simplest form, intent is your goal or purpose—the desired outcome of your spell. Whether you are casting a spell for love, protection, prosperity, or transformation, your intent must be clear, specific, and aligned with your true desires.

- **Clarity of Intent:** Before casting any spell, spend some time reflecting on what you genuinely want to achieve. A vague or conflicting intent can lead to ambiguous results. For example, if you intend to cast a spell for abundance, specify what kind of abundance you seek (financial prosperity, emotional support, creative inspiration). The clearer your intention, the more likely your spell will manifest in the way you envision.
- **Positive Intent:** Focus on what you want to bring into your life rather than what you want to avoid. For instance, instead of casting a spell to "banish loneliness," frame your intent as "attracting love and companionship." By focusing on positive outcomes, you align your energy with attraction rather than repulsion, which can lead to more harmonious results.
- **Ethical Considerations:** When setting your intent, consider the potential impact on others. The ethical principle of "harm none" is a guiding light for many practitioners. Avoid spells that manipulate, control, or harm others. Instead, focus on empowering yourself, promoting well-being, and inviting positive energy into your life.
- **Writing Your Intent:** To solidify your intention, write it down on a piece of paper before you begin your spell. This can serve as a focal point during the ritual. Use concise, affirmative

language to state your intention. For example, "I seek to attract loving and supportive relationships into my life," or "I open myself to prosperity and abundance."

2. The Power of Focus: Concentrating Your Energy

Once your intent is clear, the next step is to focus your mind and direct your energy toward that intention. Focus is the mental concentration that fuels your spell, guiding the energies of the universe to align with your desired outcome.

- **Mindfulness and Meditation:** Practicing mindfulness or meditation before spellwork can help calm your mind and sharpen your focus. Take a few moments to sit quietly, close your eyes, and breathe deeply. Visualize your intent in your mind's eye, and imagine what it will feel like when your spell manifests. This mental imagery strengthens your connection to your intention and prepares you for the spellcasting process.
- **Visualization Techniques:** Visualization is a powerful tool in magic. As you perform your spell, visualize your intention as if it has already come to pass. For example, if you are casting a spell for protection, picture yourself surrounded by a glowing shield of light. If you are casting a love spell, imagine the warmth of loving energy enveloping you. The more vividly you can imagine your desired outcome, the more energy you direct toward manifesting it.
- **Physical Gestures:** Incorporating physical actions into your spell can help focus your energy. This might include tracing symbols in the air, stirring a potion, or carving symbols into a candle. These gestures act as a bridge between your intent and the physical world, grounding your energy in your actions.
- **Mantras and Affirmations:** Repeating a mantra or affirmation during your spell can help maintain your focus. Choose words or phrases that resonate with your intention. For example, during a protection spell, you might chant, "I am safe, I am protected, I am surrounded by light." The rhythm and repetition of the mantra keep your mind centered on your intent.

3. Timing in Spellcasting: When to Cast Your Spell

Timing can significantly influence the outcome of your spellwork. While spells can be cast at any time, aligning them with certain phases of the moon, days of the week, or astrological events can amplify their power. Here's how to use timing to enhance your Samhain spells:

- **Moon Phases:** The moon's phases are deeply connected to the ebb and flow of energy. Working with these cycles can enhance the effectiveness of your spellwork.
    - **New Moon:** A time for new beginnings, setting intentions, and initiating changes. Ideal for spells related to starting new projects, personal growth, or attracting new opportunities.
    - **Waxing Moon:** As the moon grows from new to full, it brings an energy of growth and increase. This is the perfect time for spells focused on attraction, love, abundance, and manifestation.
    - **Full Moon:** The full moon represents the peak of energy and power. Spells cast during this time are highly potent and suitable for a wide range of purposes, including divination, protection, and releasing unwanted energies.
    - **Waning Moon:** As the moon decreases in light, it carries a natural energy of release and banishment. Use this phase for spells that involve letting go of negativity, breaking bad habits, or removing obstacles.
- **Days of the Week:** Each day of the week is ruled by a specific planet, which imbues it with certain energies that can support your spellwork.
    - **Monday (Moon):** Ideal for spells related to emotions, intuition, dreams, and healing.
    - **Tuesday (Mars):** Perfect for spells involving courage, strength, protection, and conflict resolution.
    - **Wednesday (Mercury):** Suitable for spells related to communication, knowledge, travel, and learning.
    - **Thursday (Jupiter):** Excellent for prosperity, abundance, luck, and growth spells.
    - **Friday (Venus):** Best for love, beauty, friendship, and harmony spells.

- ○ **Saturday (Saturn):** Ideal for banishing, protection, endings, and transformation.
- ○ **Sunday (Sun):** Great for spells focusing on success, health, vitality, and personal power.
- **Astrological Timing:** The position of the planets can add another layer of energy to your spellwork. For example, casting a love spell during a Venus transit or a protection spell when the moon is in a water sign (Cancer, Scorpio, Pisces) can enhance the effectiveness of your ritual. Some practitioners also choose to work with planetary hours, selecting specific times of day that correspond to the energies they wish to invoke.
- **Samhain's Unique Timing:** Samhain itself provides a powerful context for spellcasting. The thinning of the veil between worlds makes it an ideal time for spells related to divination, spirit communication, transformation, and releasing the past. Spells cast during Samhain carry the energy of death and rebirth, making them particularly effective for deep change and renewal.

4. The Importance of Ritual: Creating a Framework for Your Spell

A spell is more than a simple wish; it is a ritualized act that channels energy toward a specific goal. Creating a ritual framework for your spell helps structure your intention and focus your mind. Here are the key steps in a basic spellcasting ritual:

1. **Purify Your Space:** Before you begin, cleanse your space using incense, sage, or saltwater to remove any negative or stagnant energy. This purification sets the stage for your spell and ensures that the energies you work with are aligned with your intention.
2. **Cast Your Circle:** Casting a circle creates a sacred, protected space for your spellwork. This boundary separates the magical realm from the mundane, allowing you to focus your energy without interference.
3. **Call Upon the Elements:** Many practitioners invite the elements (Earth, Air, Fire, Water) to support their spellwork. Acknowledge and honor these energies as you prepare to cast your spell.

4. **State Your Intention:** Clearly state your intention out loud. Speak it as though it has already come to pass, using affirmative language. This verbal declaration solidifies your intent and sets the magical energy in motion.

5. **Perform the Spell:** Use the ingredients, tools, and gestures you have chosen to perform the spell. Whether lighting a candle, stirring a potion, or creating a sigil, each action should be performed with focused intention and visualization.

6. **Release the Energy:** Once the spell is complete, release the energy into the universe. This might involve blowing out a candle, scattering herbs into the wind, or burying a written intention in the ground. Trust that the energy will work in alignment with your intention.

7. **Close the Circle:** Thank any spirits, elements, or deities you have called upon and release them. Close the circle by visualizing the boundary dissolving back into the ether.

8. **Ground Yourself:** After spellwork, ground yourself by eating, drinking water, or holding a grounding stone like hematite. This helps you return to the physical world and release any excess energy.

5. Trust and Patience: Allowing Your Spells to Manifest

After casting your spell, it's crucial to trust in the process and allow the energy to manifest. Avoid obsessing over the outcome or repeatedly casting the same spell in a short period. This impatience can create energetic blocks that hinder your spell's effectiveness.

- **Letting Go:** Release your intention to the universe, trusting that it will unfold in the right way and at the right time. This act of surrender demonstrates confidence in your magic and the natural flow of energy.

- **Signs and Symbols:** Pay attention to signs, dreams, and synchronicities in the days and weeks following your spellwork. The universe often communicates through subtle signals, providing guidance or confirmation that your spell is working.

- **Reflect and Record:** Keep a journal of your spellcasting experiences. Record your intentions, the steps you took, and any results or signs you observe. Reflecting on your practice helps you learn what works best for you and deepens your understanding of magic.

By mastering the basics of spellcasting—understanding intent, focusing your energy, and choosing the right timing—you lay the groundwork for successful magic. As you continue to practice, you will develop a deeper intuition and confidence in your abilities, allowing you to work with the energies of Samhain and beyond to manifest your desires.

Chapter 4: Samhain Correspondences: Colors, Herbs, Crystals, Symbols, and Deities Associated with Samhain

Samhain is a festival rich in symbolism and spiritual significance, marked by a unique set of correspondences that enhance the energy of spellwork and rituals. By aligning your practice with the traditional colors, herbs, crystals, symbols, and deities associated with Samhain, you can deepen your connection to this magical season and amplify the power of your spells. This chapter will explore these correspondences in detail, providing you with the knowledge to create more intentional and effective spellwork.

1. Colors of Samhain: Channeling Seasonal Energies

Colors play a crucial role in magic, each carrying a specific vibrational frequency that influences the energy of your spellwork. During Samhain, colors not only reflect the season's natural palette but also correspond to the festival's themes of death, transformation, and the spirit world. Here are the primary colors associated with Samhain and their magical meanings:

- **Black:** A powerful color of protection, banishing, and transformation. Black is closely associated with the mysteries of the night, the void, and the unknown. During Samhain, it represents the death of the old year and the protective darkness that shelters the new beginnings to come. Use black candles, altar cloths, and crystals to create a protective boundary during your rituals, to banish negativity, or to explore the deeper mysteries of the spirit realm.
- **Orange:** Symbolizing the harvest, warmth, and vitality, orange embodies the autumnal energy of Samhain. It also represents the fire of life that continues to burn even as nature retreats into dormancy. Incorporate orange into your spells for creativity, strength, and joy. Using orange candles or pumpkins on your altar can also help attract prosperity and positive energy during this season.
- **Purple:** Purple is the color of intuition, psychic power, and spiritual connection. As Samhain is a time when the veil between worlds is thin, purple enhances divination practices, spirit communication, and the development of psychic abilities. Use purple candles, crystals, or altar decorations to channel this mystical energy, especially when seeking guidance from ancestors or exploring your inner realms.

- **Red:** Red represents the life force, passion, and the bloodline that connects us to our ancestors. During Samhain, it is used to honor those who have passed and to channel the fiery energy needed for transformation. Use red in your spellwork to tap into ancestral wisdom, ignite courage, or strengthen the bonds of love and family.
- **White:** A symbol of purity, peace, and spiritual light, white is often used during Samhain to connect with the spirit world and to honor deceased loved ones. White candles, flowers, or altar cloths can serve as offerings to spirits and ancestors, as well as tools for cleansing and protection.

2. Samhain Herbs: Harnessing the Magic of the Harvest

Herbs are a fundamental component of spellwork, each carrying unique properties that can enhance your rituals. During Samhain, the herbs associated with the season embody the energies of protection, divination, spirit communication, and transformation. Here is a list of key herbs to incorporate into your Samhain spells and rituals:

- **Mugwort:** Known for its connection to the spirit world and its ability to enhance psychic abilities, mugwort is a quintessential herb for Samhain. Use it in divination practices, dreamwork, or spirit communication rituals. Burn mugwort as incense during scrying sessions, or place it under your pillow to promote prophetic dreams.
- **Sage:** A powerful cleansing herb, sage is used to purify spaces, tools, and the self. During Samhain, burning sage helps to banish negativity, ward off malevolent spirits, and create a protective circle around your sacred space. Its purifying smoke clears the air for spiritual work and opens channels for positive energy.
- **Rosemary:** An herb of remembrance and protection, rosemary is perfect for honoring ancestors and creating a protective atmosphere for your Samhain spellwork. Add rosemary to an ancestral altar, burn it as incense, or use it in charm bags for personal protection.
- **Cinnamon:** Associated with warmth, abundance, and spiritual connection, cinnamon adds a fiery energy to your Samhain rituals. It can be used in spells for prosperity, love, and protection. Burn cinnamon sticks as an offering to spirits, or add cinnamon powder to charm bags for attracting positive energy.

- **Wormwood:** Deeply connected to spirit communication and the underworld, wormwood is an excellent herb for Samhain rituals focused on divination and contacting the spirit realm. Burn wormwood during seances, scrying, or meditation to enhance your psychic perception and open the door to the otherworld.
- **Yew:** A tree of death and rebirth, yew is associated with transformation and immortality. Its energy is potent for working with ancestors and understanding the cyclical nature of life and death. Use yew branches, leaves, or wood in spells for protection, transformation, or to honor those who have passed on.

3. Crystals for Samhain: Amplifying Spiritual Energy

Crystals are natural amplifiers of energy, each possessing specific properties that can be harnessed for spellwork. During Samhain, the crystals associated with the season resonate with themes of protection, divination, spirit communication, and transformation. Here are some powerful crystals to work with during Samhain:

- **Obsidian:** A volcanic glass known for its grounding and protective qualities, obsidian is a stone of deep transformation. It absorbs negative energies and shields against psychic attack. During Samhain, use obsidian for protection spells, scrying, and shadow work, as it helps reveal hidden truths and fosters self-awareness.
- **Amethyst:** A crystal of intuition, spiritual growth, and connection to the higher realms, amethyst is ideal for divination and spirit communication during Samhain. Place amethyst on your altar to enhance psychic abilities, or wear it to open your third eye and strengthen your connection to the spirit world.
- **Smoky Quartz:** Smoky quartz is a powerful grounding stone that absorbs negative energy and protects against spiritual interference. During Samhain, it can be used in protection rituals, cleansing practices, and spells that involve releasing old patterns or negative influences.
- **Carnelian:** A stone of vitality, courage, and creativity, carnelian helps to anchor your energy and strengthen your focus during spellwork. Use it in Samhain rituals for protection, grounding, and channeling the fiery energies of transformation and renewal.

- **Labradorite:** Known as the "stone of magic," labradorite is excellent for enhancing psychic abilities, spirit communication, and exploring the mysteries of the universe. Its iridescent glow resonates with the thinning veil between worlds during Samhain, making it a powerful tool for scrying, meditation, and contacting ancestors.

4. Symbols of Samhain: Powerful Emblems for Spellwork

Symbols are visual representations of energy and intention, often used in spellwork to focus and direct magical power. Samhain is rich with symbols that embody the themes of the season. Incorporating these symbols into your rituals, altar setup, or spellcraft can enhance your connection to the Samhain energies:

- **The Jack-o'-Lantern:** Traditionally carved from turnips or pumpkins, jack-o'-lanterns are symbols of protection and guidance. Placing a lit jack-o'-lantern on your doorstep is believed to ward off malevolent spirits and light the way for friendly souls. Carve protective symbols or runes into your jack-o'-lantern and use it as a beacon of light in your Samhain rituals.
- **Skulls:** Representing mortality, death, and the connection between the living and the dead, skulls are a potent symbol for Samhain. Decorate your altar with skulls (realistic replicas or symbolic representations) to honor ancestors and acknowledge the cycle of life and death. Skulls can also be used in meditation to explore inner mysteries and ancestral wisdom.
- **The Cauldron:** A symbol of transformation, the cauldron represents the womb of the goddess and the cycle of birth, death, and rebirth. During Samhain, use your cauldron to burn herbs, mix potions, or hold ritual fires. It serves as a vessel for your intentions and a reminder of the transformative power of magic.
- **The Pentacle:** Representing the five elements (Earth, Air, Fire, Water, Spirit) in balance, the pentacle is a powerful protective symbol. Place a pentacle on your altar to create a sacred space for your Samhain spellwork, or draw it on paper as a talisman for protection and grounding.
- **The Scythe:** A tool of the harvest and a symbol of the Grim Reaper, the scythe represents the cutting away of the old to make way for new growth. Incorporate the scythe into your Samhain rituals to release old patterns, banish negativity, and embrace transformation.

5. Deities Associated with Samhain: Divine Guides for Rituals and Spells

Samhain is a time when the presence of deities associated with death, transformation, and the otherworld is felt more strongly. Working with these deities during Samhain can provide guidance, protection, and insight. Here are some of the primary deities connected to Samhain:

- **The Morrigan (Celtic):** The Morrigan is the Celtic goddess of war, fate, and death. As a shapeshifter and a symbol of transformation, she embodies the themes of Samhain. Invoke the Morrigan for protection, strength, and guidance through the dark half of the year. She is especially powerful in spells of transformation, releasing the past, and embracing change.
- **Hecate (Greek):** Hecate is the goddess of magic, witchcraft, the moon, and the crossroads. As a guardian of the liminal spaces between life and death, she is a powerful guide during Samhain. Call upon Hecate for wisdom, protection, and guidance in exploring the mysteries of the spirit world. She is often invoked in spells related to divination, shadow work, and spiritual exploration.
- **Anubis (Egyptian):** The Egyptian god of the afterlife and protector of the dead, Anubis oversees the passage of souls to the spirit world. During Samhain, Anubis can be called upon for guidance in working with the dead, ancestor veneration, and protection during rituals that involve spirit communication.
- **Cernunnos (Celtic):** Cernunnos, the Horned God of the forest and the wild, represents the life-death-rebirth cycle of nature. As the god of fertility, animals, and the underworld, Cernunnos embodies the primal energy of Samhain. Invoke Cernunnos to connect with the natural world, honor the cycle of life, and explore the mysteries of death and rebirth.
- **Persephone (Greek):** The queen of the underworld and goddess of springtime, Persephone's journey between the worlds mirrors the themes of Samhain. Call upon Persephone for guidance in navigating transitions, embracing inner transformation, and finding strength in the dark.

By incorporating these correspondences into your Samhain practices—whether through colors, herbs, crystals, symbols, or deities—you align your magic with the energies of the season. This alignment amplifies your spellwork, deepens your connection to the spiritual realm, and allows you to harness the full power of Samhain's transformative magic.

Chapter 5: Samhain Rituals: Simple Rituals to Enhance the Spellcasting Process

Samhain, with its powerful energies and thinning veil between worlds, is a time ripe for magical rituals. While spellwork can be conducted year-round, the unique qualities of Samhain—its association with death, transformation, and the spirit world—make it an ideal period for certain rituals. Simple yet profound, these rituals can enhance your spellcasting process, whether you are seeking protection, communication with ancestors, or inner transformation.

This chapter provides a collection of accessible Samhain rituals that tap into the season's energy, designed to deepen your magical practice and bring your intentions to fruition. You do not need to be an advanced practitioner to perform these rituals; they are crafted to suit both beginners and seasoned witches alike.

1. Ancestral Altar Ritual: Honoring the Spirits of the Past

Samhain is the traditional time to honor deceased loved ones and ancestors. Building an ancestral altar and conducting a simple ritual not only pays homage to those who came before but also invites their guidance and wisdom into your life.

What You Need:

- A small table or surface to serve as an altar
- Photos, mementos, or symbols representing your ancestors
- White candle(s)
- A small bowl of water or salt
- Seasonal offerings (apples, nuts, bread, wine)
- Incense (such as frankincense or myrrh)

Steps:

1. **Cleanse the Space:** Start by cleansing your space with incense or a sage smudge stick to clear away any negative or stagnant energies.
2. **Set Up the Altar:** Arrange the photos and mementos of your ancestors on the altar. Place the white candle in the center, with the bowl of water or salt nearby as a purifying element.

Add seasonal offerings such as apples, nuts, or bread to represent the harvest and as gifts for the spirits.

3. **Light the Candle:** Light the candle as a beacon to invite the spirits of your ancestors into the space. As you do, say: "I light this flame to honor those who have come before, to guide the way for the spirits of my ancestors."

4. **Offer a Prayer or Incantation:** Speak words of remembrance and gratitude for your ancestors. You might say, "Beloved ancestors, I honor your memory and invite your presence. I offer these gifts in thanks for your guidance and protection."

5. **Make an Offering:** Place the food and drink offerings on the altar. If you wish, you can leave them there overnight or for the duration of the evening.

6. **Reflect and Listen:** Sit quietly before the altar, focusing on your breathing and allowing your mind to calm. Open yourself to any messages, feelings, or impressions from your ancestors. You might receive insights, a sense of comfort, or simply a feeling of presence.

7. **Thank the Spirits:** When you feel ready to close the ritual, thank your ancestors for their presence and guidance. Extinguish the candle, signaling the end of the ritual.

Optional: If you want to maintain the altar throughout the season, you can relight the candle each evening, offering a brief moment of remembrance and thanks.

2. Pumpkin Protection Spell: Warding Off Negative Energies

Pumpkins are a powerful symbol of Samhain and can be used to create a protective charm for your home. This simple ritual utilizes the natural protective energy of pumpkins and the power of carving symbols to create a magical barrier.

What You Need:

- A medium-sized pumpkin
- A knife for carving
- A small candle (tealight or votive)
- A marker or pencil for drawing
- Protective herbs (rosemary, sage, salt)

Steps:

1. **Cleanse the Pumpkin:** Cleanse the pumpkin by wiping it with saltwater or passing it through incense smoke. This clears away any unwanted energies.
2. **Carve a Protective Symbol:** Using the marker or pencil, draw a protective symbol or sigil on the pumpkin's surface. Common symbols include pentacles, runes (such as Algiz for protection), or even a simple cross. Once drawn, carve the symbol into the pumpkin with the knife.
3. **Hollow the Pumpkin:** Cut off the top of the pumpkin and hollow it out, removing the seeds and pulp. As you do this, visualize removing any negative energies from your space.
4. **Add Protective Herbs:** Sprinkle a mix of protective herbs (rosemary, sage, salt) inside the pumpkin. These herbs act as natural warding agents, enhancing the protective power of the charm.
5. **Light the Candle:** Place the small candle inside the pumpkin and light it. As the flame flickers, imagine it creating a barrier of light around your home, shielding it from negative energies and harmful influences.
6. **Recite a Protective Incantation:** Say the following (or create your own): "By flame and herb, I set this ward. Let no ill will pass through this light. I call upon the spirit of Samhain to guard this place, to keep it safe and whole."
7. **Place the Pumpkin:** Place the carved pumpkin outside your front door, on a windowsill, or in a location where it can serve as a guardian for your home. Allow the candle to burn as long as it is safe to do so.

3. Divination Ritual: Seeking Guidance for the Year Ahead

Samhain is an excellent time for divination, as the veil between worlds is at its thinnest, allowing for clearer communication with the spiritual realm. This ritual uses tarot cards, runes, or another form of divination to gain insight into the coming year.

What You Need:

- Tarot deck, runes, or a scrying mirror
- A purple or black candle (for intuition)

- Incense (mugwort or sandalwood)
- A quiet, undisturbed space

Steps:

1. **Prepare the Space:** Cleanse your space by burning incense. Set up a small altar with your divination tools and light the candle to represent the spiritual light guiding your reading.
2. **Set Your Intent:** Sit quietly and take a few deep breaths. Focus on your intention for the divination. This could be to gain general guidance for the coming year, insight into a specific question, or messages from your spirit guides.
3. **Perform the Divination:** Shuffle your tarot deck or cast your runes, allowing your intuition to guide you. As you lay out the cards or interpret the runes, remain open to any impressions, feelings, or messages that come through.
4. **Interpret the Results:** Take your time to interpret the symbols, images, or messages. If using tarot, consider pulling a single card for each month of the upcoming year, reflecting on the energy each card represents. For runes, you might cast three runes for past, present, and future insights.
5. **Record Your Reading:** Write down your interpretations in a journal to revisit throughout the year. This record can provide valuable insights and guidance as the seasons change.
6. **Thank the Spirits:** When you have completed the reading, thank the spiritual energies and guides that assisted you. Extinguish the candle to close the ritual.

4. Banishing Ritual: Releasing What No Longer Serves You

Samhain marks the end of the harvest and the beginning of the darker half of the year, making it an ideal time for releasing unwanted energies, habits, or relationships. This simple ritual uses the element of fire to banish what you wish to release.

What You Need:

- A black candle (for banishing)
- A piece of paper and pen

- A fireproof bowl or cauldron
- Sage or rosemary for burning

Steps:

1. **Set Up Your Space:** Create a calm and quiet atmosphere by lighting the black candle. Place the fireproof bowl on your altar or a safe surface.
2. **Reflect:** Spend a few moments reflecting on what you wish to release. This could be negative habits, emotional baggage, toxic relationships, or anything that no longer serves your well-being.
3. **Write It Down:** On the piece of paper, write down the things you are ready to let go of. Be honest and specific, acknowledging how these things have affected you.
4. **Burn the Paper:** Hold the paper over the candle flame (with caution) and let it catch fire. Place it into the fireproof bowl or cauldron to burn completely. As the paper burns, visualize the unwanted energies dissolving and transforming into smoke, rising away from you.
5. **Say an Incantation:** Recite an incantation, such as: "By the light of this flame, I release what no longer serves. From my life, let it be gone, to return no more."
6. **Cleanse the Space:** After the paper has burned, cleanse the space with sage or rosemary, allowing the smoke to purify the area and fill it with positive energy.
7. **Close the Ritual:** Extinguish the candle, signaling the end of the ritual. Take a moment to ground yourself by breathing deeply or holding a grounding stone like hematite.

5. The Cauldron of Transformation: Embracing Change

This ritual uses the cauldron—a powerful symbol of transformation—to release the past and set intentions for the new cycle. It's perfect for those who wish to embrace change and welcome new opportunities into their lives.

What You Need:

- A small cauldron or fireproof bowl
- A piece of paper and pen

- Bay leaves (for wishes and intentions)
- A lighter or matches
- Herbs associated with change (such as mint or basil)

Steps:

1. **Prepare Your Space:** Cleanse your space with sage or incense and set up your cauldron on your altar. Surround it with bay leaves and herbs that resonate with the energy of change.
2. **Set Your Intentions:** On the piece of paper, write down what you are ready to let go of and what you wish to manifest in its place. Be specific about the changes you want to invite into your life.
3. **Burn the Paper:** Fold the paper and place it in the cauldron. Light it with a match or lighter, allowing it to burn. As the flames consume the paper, visualize the release of old energies and the infusion of new, positive energy.
4. **Add the Bay Leaves:** One by one, add the bay leaves to the flames, speaking your intentions aloud as you do. For example, "I welcome love," "I embrace prosperity," or "I invite growth."
5. **Add Herbs for Change:** Sprinkle herbs such as mint or basil into the cauldron as an offering to the universe, enhancing the transformative power of your intentions.
6. **Close the Ritual:** Once the flames have burned out, thank the cauldron for holding your intentions and the energies of Samhain for supporting your transformation. Ground yourself and extinguish any candles used in the ritual.

These simple yet profound rituals are designed to align you with the energies of Samhain, enhancing your spellcasting process. Whether you are honoring ancestors, seeking guidance, banishing negativity, or embracing transformation, these rituals provide a foundation for deepening your magical practice during this powerful time of year.

Part I: Love Spells (1-200)

Chapter 6: Love Attraction Spells (1-50): Spells to Attract New Love

Samhain is a powerful time for magic, and its energy can be harnessed to draw new love into your life. During this season, the veil between the worlds is thin, and the natural energies are ripe for spellwork focused on attraction, romance, and matters of the heart. This chapter features 50 spells specifically designed to attract new love, including simple charms, rituals, and more elaborate spells that use the symbolic elements of autumn.

Whether you're seeking a deep romantic connection, the excitement of a new crush, or simply an open heart ready to receive love, these spells align with Samhain's energies of transformation and renewal. Let's explore these love attraction spells in detail, beginning with two signature spells: "Autumn Romance Charm" and "Harvest Heart Magnet."

1. Autumn Romance Charm

The "Autumn Romance Charm" uses the magic of autumn leaves to attract a new love. As the leaves change colors and fall, they symbolize change and new beginnings, making them ideal for this spell.

What You Need:

- A small, red or orange autumn leaf (symbolizing love and passion)
- A pink candle (representing love)
- Rose petals (fresh or dried)
- A small pouch or sachet
- Essential oil (rose or lavender)
- A piece of rose quartz

Steps:

1. **Prepare Your Space:** Light the pink candle and place the leaf, rose petals, and rose quartz on your altar. Create a calm and focused environment by burning rose or lavender incense.
2. **Anoint the Leaf:** Anoint the autumn leaf with a few drops of rose or lavender essential oil while visualizing the type of love you wish to attract. Imagine the leaf glowing with a warm, pink light, filled with love and attraction.
3. **Set Your Intention:** Hold the leaf in your hands and state your intention out loud. For example, say, "As the leaves change and fall, I call forth love to fill my life. May new romance find its way to me."
4. **Create the Charm:** Place the anointed leaf, rose petals, and rose quartz into the pouch or sachet. As you do this, visualize your heart opening to receive love and imagine your future lover being drawn to you.
5. **Seal the Charm:** Knot the pouch closed, sealing your intention within it. Blow out the candle and carry the charm with you, or place it under your pillow to invite love into your life.

2. Harvest Heart Magnet

The "Harvest Heart Magnet" spell uses the energy of the autumn harvest to attract love. It combines the abundance of the harvest with symbols of the heart, making it a potent spell for drawing new romantic possibilities.

What You Need:

- A small pumpkin or gourd (symbolizing abundance)
- A piece of red paper
- A red pen
- A pink ribbon
- Honey (to sweeten love)
- A handful of sunflower seeds

Steps:

1. **Prepare Your Space:** Sit quietly in your sacred space. Place the pumpkin, paper, ribbon, and other ingredients in front of you. Light a candle (pink or red) to create a warm, inviting atmosphere.

2. **Write Your Intention:** On the piece of red paper, write down the qualities you wish to attract in a lover. Be specific, focusing on traits that resonate with your true desires, such as kindness, humor, passion, or stability.

3. **Infuse the Paper with Energy:** Fold the paper in half and hold it in your hands. Close your eyes and visualize a warm, golden light surrounding the paper, filling it with the energy of love and attraction.

4. **Prepare the Pumpkin:** Cut a small slit or opening in the pumpkin. Gently pour a small amount of honey into the pumpkin, saying, "As this honey sweetens, so shall my love life attract the sweetest romance."

5. **Place the Paper and Seeds:** Place the folded paper and sunflower seeds into the pumpkin. Sunflower seeds represent growth and the blossoming of new opportunities. Imagine your love life growing and flourishing like a bountiful harvest.

6. **Seal the Pumpkin:** Use the pink ribbon to tie around the pumpkin, sealing the spell and your intention inside. As you tie the ribbon, say, "By the power of harvest and heart, love shall come to me."

7. **Place the Pumpkin:** Place the pumpkin on your altar or in a place where it will not be disturbed. Allow the energies of the spell to work, drawing love toward you as the pumpkin continues to represent abundance and attraction.

3-50. Additional Love Attraction Spells

Here are 48 more spells to attract love, ranging from simple charms to more elaborate rituals. These spells use the magical correspondences of Samhain, such as autumn leaves, pumpkins, candles, and herbs, to draw love into your life.

3. Heart of the Forest Spell

- Gather an acorn and a piece of rose quartz. Hold them together, visualizing your heart's desires. Bury the acorn in the forest, keeping the rose quartz with you to attract new love.

4. Apple of Love Ritual

- Cut an apple in half and place a heart-shaped charm inside. Bind the apple back together with a pink ribbon while focusing on the love you wish to draw into your life.

5. Crimson Leaf Attraction

- Select a red autumn leaf and write your name and the qualities you seek in a lover on it. Burn the leaf in a candle flame, sending your desires into the universe.

6. Candlelit Love Invocation

- Light a pink candle and carve a heart into it. As it burns, repeat an incantation calling for love to enter your life.

7. Samhain Love Lantern

- Create a small lantern using a carved-out pumpkin. Place a pink candle inside and light it on Samhain night to guide love to your doorstep.

8. Rosewater Love Wash

- Create a love wash using rose petals and moon-charged water. Bathe with it on the night of Samhain to cleanse your aura and attract love.

9. Seed of Affection Charm

- Place a handful of pumpkin seeds into a small bag. Anoint them with rose oil while visualizing love sprouting in your life.

10. Love's Whisper Incantation

- On a windy Samhain evening, go outside and whisper your desire for love into the wind, releasing it to the universe.

11. Autumn Fire Love Spell

- Write the qualities of your ideal partner on a piece of paper. Burn it in an autumn bonfire while chanting an incantation for love.

12. Harvest Honey Jar

- Create a honey jar spell with herbs and flowers associated with love. Seal your intention within the jar to sweeten your love life.

13. Love Apple Charm

- Carve your initials and a heart into an apple. Eat it on Samhain night, visualizing love filling your life with each bite.

14. The Lovers' Knot

- Braid a pink, red, and white ribbon while focusing on the love you wish to attract. Keep the braided ribbon under your pillow.

15. Moonlit Mirror Love Reflection

- Place a small mirror under the light of the waxing moon. In the morning, look into the mirror and visualize love finding you.

16. Cinnamon Heart Attraction Pouch
What You Need:

- A small red or pink pouch
- Cinnamon sticks (representing warmth and attraction)
- A rose petal (symbolizing love)
- A small piece of garnet or rose quartz

Steps:

1. **Prepare the Ingredients:** Gather the cinnamon sticks, rose petal, and gemstone. Visualize these items glowing with the energy of love.
2. **Fill the Pouch:** Place the cinnamon sticks, rose petal, and gemstone inside the pouch. As you add each item, say, "With cinnamon's warmth, love shall find me. With the rose's beauty, I attract love freely."
3. **Empower the Pouch:** Hold the pouch in your hands and close your eyes. Imagine your heart radiating with love, attracting a partner who resonates with your desires.
4. **Carry or Sleep With It:** Carry this pouch with you or place it under your pillow at night to attract new love into your life.

17. The Enchanted Harvest Spell
What You Need:

- A small pumpkin
- Honey
- Rose petals
- A red ribbon

Steps:

1. **Prepare the Pumpkin:** Carve a small opening in the pumpkin's top and scoop out the seeds.
2. **Fill with Love Symbols:** Add honey and rose petals into the hollow pumpkin, saying, "As this pumpkin holds sweetness, so shall my heart attract love."
3. **Seal the Pumpkin:** Tie the red ribbon around the pumpkin and place it on your altar. Leave it for one full moon cycle, allowing it to draw loving energy toward you.

18. Samhain Rose Water Bath
What You Need:

- Rose petals
- A bowl of water
- A few drops of rose oil
- Pink candle

Steps:

1. **Create Rose Water:** Add rose petals and a few drops of rose oil to the bowl of water.
2. **Infuse with Intention:** Light the pink candle and, as it burns, stir the water gently, focusing on the love you wish to attract.

3. **Bathtime:** Pour this rose water into your bath and soak in it on the night of Samhain, visualizing the water filling you with love and attraction.

19. Apple and Cinnamon Attraction Spell
What You Need:

- An apple
- Ground cinnamon
- A pink candle

Steps:

1. **Cut the Apple:** Cut the apple in half horizontally, revealing the star shape in its center.
2. **Sprinkle with Cinnamon:** Sprinkle cinnamon on both halves, imagining that the spice ignites the warmth of love.
3. **Light the Candle:** Light the pink candle and say, "As I taste this apple's sweetness, may love come to me in equal measure."
4. **Eat the Apple:** Eat the apple while focusing on your desire to attract a loving partner.

20. Lovers' Scrying Mirror Spell
What You Need:

- A small mirror
- A red candle
- Rose petals

Steps:

1. **Prepare the Mirror:** Place the mirror on your altar with the red candle and rose petals around it.

2. **Light the Candle:** Light the candle and gaze into the mirror's reflection.
3. **Visualize Your Lover:** As you look into the mirror, imagine the qualities you seek in a partner. See them standing beside you in the reflection.
4. **Seal the Vision:** Blow out the candle, capturing the image in the mirror. Keep the mirror on your altar as a magnet for the love you visualized.

21. Samhain Love Letter Ritual
What You Need:

- A piece of pink paper
- A red or pink pen
- Rose petals
- A pink envelope

Steps:

1. **Write the Letter:** Write a letter to the universe detailing the kind of love you want to attract.
2. **Fold and Seal:** Fold the letter and sprinkle it with rose petals. Place it inside the pink envelope.
3. **Seal with Intent:** Hold the envelope to your heart, saying, "As this letter is sealed, so is my wish for love."
4. **Keep It Safe:** Place the envelope under your pillow or in a special box to allow the energy to manifest.

22. Lovers' Knot Charm
What You Need:

- A pink, red, and white ribbon
- A rose quartz stone

Steps:

1. **Braid the Ribbons:** While braiding the ribbons together, focus on your desire to attract love.
2. **Wrap the Stone:** Wrap the rose quartz with the braided ribbon, saying, "With this knot, I tie the energy of love to me."
3. **Carry It:** Carry this charm with you as a magnet for love.

23. Harvest Love Jar
What You Need:

- A small jar
- Honey
- Rose petals
- A pink candle

Steps:

1. **Fill the Jar:** Add honey and rose petals to the jar, representing sweetness and love.
2. **Seal with Wax:** Light the pink candle and pour a bit of wax over the jar's lid to seal it.
3. **Speak Your Intention:** Say, "As this jar is sealed, may love come to me, sweet and true."
4. **Keep the Jar:** Place the jar on your altar to draw in loving energy.

24. Apple Seed Attraction Ritual
What You Need:

- An apple
- A piece of pink paper
- A pen
- A garden or pot of soil

Steps:

1. **Cut the Apple:** Cut the apple and remove the seeds.
2. **Write Your Intention:** Write your desire for love on the piece of pink paper.
3. **Plant the Seeds:** Wrap the seeds in the paper and plant them in the soil, saying, "As these seeds grow, so shall love find me."
4. **Water the Plant:** Water the soil, nurturing the seeds as a symbol of your love growing.

25. The Rose Moon Spell
What You Need:

- A pink candle
- Rose petals
- A piece of moon-charged water

Steps:

1. **Prepare the Altar:** Place the rose petals around the pink candle on your altar.
2. **Light the Candle:** Light the candle and pour a small amount of moon-charged water into a bowl.
3. **Reflect the Moon:** Hold the bowl up to the moonlight, saying, "By the light of the moon, I attract love into my life."
4. **Wash Your Hands:** Dip your hands in the moon water and wash them, symbolizing readiness to receive love.

26-50. Additional Love Attraction Spells

Here is a brief overview of more love spells tailored for the Samhain season:

26. Red Ribbon Attraction Knot – Tie nine knots in a red ribbon, focusing on love with each knot.

27. Lavender Love Bath – Add lavender petals and essential oil to your bath to attract calm and gentle love.

28. The Lovers' Amulet – Create an amulet using a rose quartz crystal and wear it to draw love.

29. Autumn Rose Sachet – Fill a sachet with dried rose petals, carry it in your pocket to attract romantic energy.

30. Sweet Dreams Pillow Spell – Place rose petals and a sprig of lavender under your pillow to dream of your future love.

31. Love's Ember Ritual – Write your desire for love on a bay leaf and burn it in a fireproof dish on Samhain night.

32. Apple Blossom Candle Magic – Carve a heart into an apple-scented candle and let it burn to attract romance.

33. Autumn Wind Whisper – Go outside on a windy day, speak your desires to the wind, and release them.

34. Pumpkin Spice Attraction – Place a cinnamon stick and clove inside a hollowed pumpkin; light a candle inside to attract passion.

35. Lovers' Knot Bracelet – Braid a bracelet from red thread, wear it to attract love.

36. Sweet Harvest Spell – Fill a small jar with honey and rose petals, keep it on your altar for sweet romance.

37. Apple Blossom Love Tea – Brew tea with apple blossoms and drink it to enhance your love-attracting aura.

38. The First Frost Spell – On the first frost of Samhain morning, go outside, gather a leaf, and speak your desire into it.

39. Lovers' Charm Bag – Fill a small bag with rose petals, rosemary, and cinnamon. Keep it close to draw in new love.

40. Lovers' Quartz Ritual – Hold a piece of rose quartz under the Samhain moon, infusing it with love energy.

41. Honeyed Love Spell – Write your intention for love on a piece of paper, anoint it with honey, and bury it in your garden.

42. Autumn Leaf Love Drawing – Write your name on a fallen leaf and keep it on your altar until love finds you.

43. Lovers' Mirror Ritual – Place a mirror on your altar, surrounded by rose petals. Look into it each night, imagining love.

44. Love Knot Sachet – Tie nine knots in a piece of red thread and place it in a sachet with rose petals.

45. The Lovers' Lantern – Carve a small pumpkin into a lantern, place a pink candle inside to draw love.

46. Rose Quartz Attraction Ring – Wear a rose quartz ring on your finger to attract romantic connections.

47. The Lovers' Call – At dusk, light a pink candle, whisper your desire into the flame, and let the candle burn.

48. Lovers' Cup Tea Ritual – Brew tea with rose petals and drink it while envisioning the love you wish to attract.

49. Samhain Lovers' Sigil – Create a sigil representing love, draw it on a piece of paper, and place it under a pink candle.

50. The Autumn Heart Spell – On a heart-shaped leaf, write down your intention for love. Place it under your pillow to draw love to you in dreams.

These spells utilize the magical energies of Samhain, the changing season, and the symbols of autumn to attract love into your life. Perform them with a clear heart, positive intentions, and an open mind to the possibilities that the universe holds. As you cast these spells, trust that the love you seek is already on its way to you, drawn by the power of your intention and the magic of the season.

Love Attraction Spell Structure

When casting love spells, keep in mind a few key principles:

- **Clarity:** Be clear about the qualities you desire in a partner. Focus on the type of relationship you wish to cultivate, rather than specific individuals.
- **Positivity:** Frame your intentions in positive language. Instead of asking for what you don't want, focus on the attributes and feelings you wish to attract.
- **Timing:** Many love spells are best cast during the waxing moon phase or on the night of Samhain when the energies for transformation and attraction are at their peak.
- **Grounding:** After performing love spells, it's important to ground yourself to avoid becoming overly preoccupied with the outcome. Trust that the energy you've sent out will work in harmony with the universe.

By using these 50 love attraction spells, you can tap into the magic of Samhain to open your heart, attract romantic opportunities, and invite the love you desire into your life. Remember, the most powerful love spells are those cast with an open heart, a clear mind, and respect for the free will of others. May your journey into the realm of romance be as enchanting as the season of Samhain itself.

Chapter 7: Self-Love Spells (51-100): Spells to Promote Self-Acceptance and Self-Care

Samhain is not only a time to connect with others and attract new love, but it also offers a powerful opportunity to turn inward, embracing self-love and self-care. In the dim light of autumn and the quiet introspection of Samhain, we find the perfect setting for nurturing our inner selves. The spells in this chapter are designed to foster self-acceptance, boost self-worth, and create a strong foundation of self-care. By aligning with the transformative energy of Samhain, these spells guide you in cultivating a loving relationship with yourself.

Each spell focuses on a different aspect of self-love, using elements of the season such as candles, herbs, crystals, and the natural beauty of autumn. This chapter includes 50 self-love spells, including the featured "Mirror of Self-Compassion" and "Autumn Self-Worth Booster," to empower you on your journey toward inner harmony and self-acceptance.

51. Mirror of Self-Compassion

This spell uses the reflective power of a mirror to help you embrace self-compassion and speak words of kindness to yourself.

What You Need:

- A small hand mirror
- A pink candle (for self-love)
- Rose petals (fresh or dried)
- A piece of rose quartz (optional)

Steps:

1. **Set Up Your Space:** Cleanse your space with incense or sage, and place the mirror on your altar or a small table. Surround it with rose petals and the rose quartz.
2. **Light the Candle:** Light the pink candle, symbolizing the warmth of self-love and compassion.
3. **Gaze into the Mirror:** Sit comfortably and gaze into the mirror. Look deeply into your own eyes, acknowledging the person looking back at you.

4. **Speak Words of Kindness:** Begin speaking words of self-compassion out loud, such as, "I am worthy of love," "I accept myself as I am," or "I forgive myself for past mistakes." Feel the power of these words resonate within you as you repeat them.
5. **Visualize Self-Love:** As you speak, visualize a warm pink light surrounding you, filling you with love, compassion, and acceptance.
6. **Seal the Energy:** When you feel ready, blow out the candle, symbolizing the sealing of this energy within you. Carry the rose quartz with you as a reminder of this ritual.

52. Autumn Self-Worth Booster

This spell harnesses the energy of autumn leaves to help you boost your self-worth, reminding you that just as nature changes, so can your perception of yourself.

What You Need:

- A small, colorful autumn leaf
- A piece of paper and a pen
- A pink ribbon
- Cinnamon powder (for warmth and confidence)

Steps:

1. **Write Your Intentions:** On the piece of paper, write down qualities you admire about yourself and things you are proud of. Fold the paper and hold it in your hands.
2. **Anoint the Leaf:** Sprinkle a pinch of cinnamon on the autumn leaf, saying, "As this leaf changes and falls, so do I grow in self-worth and confidence."
3. **Create the Bundle:** Wrap the leaf and paper together with the pink ribbon, tying a knot to seal your intentions within it.
4. **Carry the Charm:** Carry this charm with you or place it on your altar to remind you of your self-worth. Whenever you need a boost, hold the charm and read the words you wrote.

53. Candlelit Self-Love Ritual
What You Need:

- A pink candle
- Rose oil
- A small bowl of water
- Rose petals

Steps:

1. **Anoint the Candle:** Rub rose oil on the pink candle, infusing it with your intention for self-love.
2. **Set Up Your Space:** Place the candle in the center of your altar, surrounded by the bowl of water and rose petals.
3. **Light the Candle:** Light the candle and gaze into the flame, visualizing the warmth of self-love filling your heart.
4. **Reflect:** As the candle burns, reflect on your qualities, achievements, and things you love about yourself. Speak them out loud if you wish.
5. **Dip Your Hands:** Dip your hands in the bowl of water, symbolizing the cleansing of negative self-perceptions. Allow yourself to feel renewed and loved.

54. Rose Quartz Heart Healing Spell
What You Need:

- A rose quartz crystal
- A small piece of paper
- A pink ribbon

Steps:

1. **Write Your Affirmation:** On the paper, write an affirmation such as, "I am worthy of love and kindness."
2. **Wrap the Crystal:** Place the rose quartz on the paper and fold the paper around it. Tie the pink ribbon around the bundle, sealing your intention inside.
3. **Hold the Crystal:** Whenever you need a reminder of your self-worth, hold the crystal and repeat your affirmation.

55. Self-Care Bath Ritual
What You Need:

- Rose petals
- Lavender essential oil
- Sea salt
- Pink candle

Steps:

1. **Prepare the Bath:** Draw a warm bath and add rose petals, lavender oil, and sea salt to the water.
2. **Light the Candle:** Light the pink candle and place it safely nearby. Allow its gentle glow to create a calming atmosphere.
3. **Soak and Reflect:** Soak in the bath, visualizing the water washing away self-doubt and filling you with peace and self-love.
4. **Affirm:** As you relax, repeat affirmations like, "I am deserving of care and kindness."

56. Autumn Wind Release

What You Need:

- A piece of paper
- A pen
- An autumn leaf

Steps:

1. **Write Your Negative Thoughts:** On the paper, write down any self-doubts, fears, or negative thoughts you hold about yourself.
2. **Go Outside:** Take the paper and leaf outside on a breezy day. Hold the paper in your hands and, with eyes closed, say, "I release these doubts to the autumn wind, to be carried away and transformed."
3. **Burn the Paper:** Safely burn the paper and let the ashes scatter in the wind, symbolizing the release of negativity.
4. **Hold the Leaf:** Hold the autumn leaf close to your heart, breathing in its grounding energy, and say, "I embrace myself as I am."

57. Heartwarming Apple Spell

What You Need:

- An apple
- Honey
- A small knife

Steps:

1. **Cut the Apple:** Cut the apple in half horizontally, revealing the star shape in its center.

2. **Anoint with Honey:** Drizzle honey over the apple halves, saying, "As this apple holds sweetness, so do I hold love for myself."
3. **Eat the Apple:** Eat the apple, feeling the sweetness fill you with love and acceptance.

58. Self-Love Knot Ritual
What You Need:

- A pink or red ribbon

Steps:

1. **Set Your Intention:** Hold the ribbon and focus on your intention for self-love.
2. **Tie Nine Knots:** As you tie each knot, say an affirmation such as, "I am worthy of love," "I accept myself," or "I am enough."
3. **Carry the Ribbon:** Keep the ribbon with you as a reminder of the self-love you've woven into your life.

59. Samhain Self-Care Jar
What You Need:

- A small jar
- Rose petals
- Lavender
- Sea salt
- A piece of rose quartz

Steps:

1. **Fill the Jar:** Add rose petals, lavender, sea salt, and rose quartz to the jar. Each ingredient represents love, peace, and self-care.

2. **Seal the Jar:** Hold the jar in your hands and say, "I create this jar to hold love, care, and compassion for myself."

3. **Keep It Close:** Place the jar on your altar or in a place where you will see it daily as a reminder to care for and love yourself.

60-100. Additional Self-Love Spells

Here are brief overviews of more self-love spells tailored for Samhain:

60. Autumn Leaves of Love – Collect five colorful leaves, write a self-affirmation on each, and place them on your altar.

61. Sweet Dreams Self-Love Sachet – Fill a sachet with rose petals, lavender, and rosemary, and place it under your pillow for restful, self-loving dreams.

62. Morning Dew Affirmation – Collect morning dew on a piece of rose quartz and use it to anoint your heart chakra, filling yourself with love.

63. Candlelit Gratitude Ritual – Light a pink candle each morning for seven days, listing things you love about yourself.

64. Self-Care Teacup – Brew tea with rose petals and drink it while focusing on self-acceptance and care.

65. Rose-Infused Mirror Spell – Rub rose petals on a mirror, then look into it, speaking words of love to your reflection.

66. Self-Love Anointing Oil – Mix rose oil with lavender oil, anoint your wrists and heart area to promote self-compassion.

67. Autumn Acorn of Strength – Carry an acorn as a talisman of inner strength and self-worth.

68. Self-Affirmation Jar – Write positive affirmations on slips of paper, place them in a jar, and read one daily.

69. Gratitude Leaf Spell – Write things you're grateful for about yourself on a leaf and keep it in your journal.

70. Self-Care Candle Spell – Carve your name into a pink candle, light it while focusing on self-care.

71. Lavender Self-Love Bath – Create a bath with lavender and rose petals for self-care and relaxation.

72. Heart-Centered Meditation – Hold a rose quartz over your heart chakra and meditate, visualizing love filling your entire being.

73. Self-Worth Crystal Grid – Arrange crystals (rose quartz, amethyst, carnelian) in a grid on your altar to enhance self-worth.

74. Warmth of Self-Love Tea – Brew cinnamon and honey tea, drink it with the intention of warming your heart with self-love.

75. Knot of Acceptance – Tie knots in a ribbon while stating affirmations of self-acceptance.

76. Rose Petal Reflection – Place rose petals in a bowl of water, look into it, and speak affirmations.

77. Self-Worth Stone – Carry a piece of carnelian to boost confidence and self-esteem.

78. Gratitude Seed Planting – Plant seeds in a pot while speaking words of gratitude for yourself.

79. Lunar Self-Love Ritual – During a waxing moon, write a self-affirmation on paper, burn it in a candle flame to release negativity.

80. Heart-Centered Charm – Create a charm bag with rose quartz, lavender, and rose petals, carry it to remind you of your worth.

81. Samhain Self-Love Bath Bomb – Create a bath bomb with rose and lavender oils, use it during a self-care bath.

82. Self-Love Tarot Reading – Draw three tarot cards to explore areas of self-care, self-love, and acceptance.

83. Self-Worth Knot Talisman – Tie a knot in a ribbon each day for seven days while stating a self-love affirmation.

84. Rose Quartz Meditation – Hold a piece of rose quartz in your hand during meditation to focus on self-love.

85. Gratitude Pebble Spell – Carry a small pebble in your pocket; each time you touch it, remind yourself of one thing you love about yourself.

86. Heart-Centered Breathwork – Sit comfortably, focus on deep breathing while holding a rose quartz over your heart.

87. Self-Care Jar – Fill a jar with slips of paper, each containing an act of self-care; draw one whenever you need to practice self-love.

88. Love Letter to Self – Write a love letter to yourself, detailing your qualities and strengths; keep it in a special place.

89. Self-Compassion Candle – Light a pink candle whenever you feel self-critical, focusing on self-compassion as it burns.

90. Mirror Affection – Each morning, look in the mirror and say three things you love about yourself.

91. Self-Worth Bracelet – Create a beaded bracelet with rose quartz and wear it as a reminder of your self-worth.

92. Full Moon Self-Love Bath – On the full moon, take a bath with sea salt and rose petals to cleanse and fill yourself with self-love.

93. Heart-Centered Spell Jar – Create a small jar with rose petals, lavender, and a piece of rose quartz, seal it as a talisman of love.

94. Morning Dew Self-Care Ritual – Collect morning dew, anoint your forehead and heart, affirming self-love.

95. Knot of Compassion – Tie a knot in a red ribbon while stating a self-compassionate affirmation.

96. Heart-Centered Journal – Start a journal, writing one thing you love about yourself each day.

97. Candle of Self-Acceptance – Light a candle, gaze into the flame, and affirm your worthiness of love and care.

98. Heart-Healing Crystal Grid – Arrange crystals in a heart shape on your altar, focusing on self-love.

99. Self-Care Affirmation Charm – Write affirmations on paper slips, place them in a small pouch, carry it as a reminder of self-love.

100. The Autumn Embrace Spell – Hold an autumn leaf close to your heart, visualizing it filling you with love and acceptance.

These self-love spells are designed to be nurturing, gentle, and empowering, using the energy of Samhain to promote self-acceptance, compassion, and care. By practicing these rituals, you open the door to a deeper understanding of your worth and create a loving relationship with yourself.

Chapter 8: Relationship Harmony Spells (101-150): Spells to Strengthen Existing Relationships

Samhain, with its transformative energy and thinning of the veil between worlds, is an opportune time to enhance the bonds of existing relationships. The season's energy can be channeled to promote harmony, understanding, forgiveness, and deeper emotional connection between partners, friends, or family members. These relationship harmony spells focus on creating a balanced and loving dynamic, easing tensions, and fostering a sense of unity and respect.

This chapter provides 50 spells designed to nurture and strengthen relationships, including specific spells like "Bonding Under the Moon" and "Samhain Reconciliation Ritual." Each spell draws upon the elements and symbols of the season, using tools such as candles, herbs, crystals, and the power of intention to harmonize and balance the energies within your relationships.

101. Bonding Under the Moon

This spell uses the calming and unifying energy of the moon to strengthen the emotional bond between you and a loved one. It is ideal for partners, close friends, or family members.

What You Need:

- Two pink candles (symbolizing love and unity)
- A piece of rose quartz
- A small bowl of water
- A sprig of rosemary (for healing and protection)

Steps:

1. **Prepare Your Space:** On the night of a full or waxing moon, cleanse your space with sage or rosemary incense. Place the candles, rose quartz, and bowl of water on your altar or a small table.
2. **Light the Candles:** Light the two pink candles, representing you and your loved one. As you light each candle, say, "By the light of the moon, may the bond between us grow in love and harmony."

3. **Add the Rosemary to the Water:** Place the rosemary sprig into the bowl of water. This represents the cleansing of any negativity in the relationship and the promotion of mutual understanding.
4. **Hold the Rose Quartz:** Hold the rose quartz in your hand, visualizing the moonlight shining down upon you and your loved one, enveloping you both in a warm, unifying light.
5. **Speak Your Intention:** Speak aloud your desire for harmony in the relationship. For example, "May our hearts beat as one, in understanding, trust, and love."
6. **Extinguish the Candles:** Gently blow out the candles, releasing your intention to the universe. Keep the rose quartz near your bedside or in a shared space as a reminder of your bond.

102. Samhain Reconciliation Ritual

The "Samhain Reconciliation Ritual" is designed to help heal and mend relationships strained by misunderstandings, arguments, or emotional distance. This ritual uses the transformative energy of Samhain to clear the air and invite harmony back into the relationship.

What You Need:

- A small pumpkin or gourd
- A piece of paper and pen
- A black candle (to absorb negativity)
- A pink or white candle (to restore harmony)
- Rosemary and sage (for healing and purification)
- A pink ribbon

Steps:

1. **Cleanse Your Space:** Begin by cleansing your space with sage to remove negative energies. Place the pumpkin, candles, paper, and herbs on your altar.
2. **Write Your Intention:** On the piece of paper, write down the names of the people involved and the words, "I release all negativity and open my heart to forgiveness and harmony."

3. **Carve a Small Slit:** Using a knife, carve a small slit in the pumpkin. Place the folded paper inside the pumpkin, visualizing the negative energy being absorbed and transformed by the pumpkin.
4. **Light the Black Candle:** Light the black candle, focusing on releasing the conflict and tension from the relationship. Say, "As this candle burns, so does all discord and negativity fade away."
5. **Light the Pink or White Candle:** Light the second candle, representing the restoration of peace and harmony. Say, "As this flame shines, may love and understanding fill our hearts anew."
6. **Tie the Ribbon:** Wrap the pink ribbon around the pumpkin, tying it in a knot. This act symbolizes binding the relationship with love and unity.
7. **Place the Pumpkin:** Place the pumpkin outside your home or on your altar. Allow the candles to burn down safely as a symbol of reconciliation.

103. Autumn Leaf Peace Charm

What You Need:

- A colorful autumn leaf
- A piece of pink ribbon
- Rose oil (for love and harmony)

Steps:

1. **Anoint the Leaf:** Dab a small amount of rose oil onto the leaf, saying, "This leaf carries peace and love between us."
2. **Tie the Ribbon:** Tie the pink ribbon around the leaf to hold your intention.
3. **Place the Charm:** Place the charm in a shared space, such as under your bed or in a living room, to promote peace and harmony.

104. Heart-Soothing Honey Jar
What You Need:

- A small jar
- Honey
- A piece of paper
- Pink candle

Steps:

1. **Write Your Intention:** On the paper, write the names of those involved and the words, "Sweeten our hearts with understanding and love."
2. **Fill the Jar:** Place the paper in the jar and fill it with honey.
3. **Seal and Light:** Seal the jar and light the pink candle, allowing a few drops of wax to seal the jar further. Say, "As this honey sweetens, so do our hearts."

105. Amethyst Connection Spell
What You Need:

- Two pieces of amethyst
- A pink ribbon

Steps:

1. **Cleanse the Crystals:** Cleanse the amethyst pieces with sage or incense.
2. **Hold the Amethyst:** Hold each piece, focusing on the bond between you and your loved one.
3. **Tie Together:** Tie the amethyst pieces together with the pink ribbon, saying, "By this knot, our connection strengthens and our hearts grow closer."

106. Candle of Forgiveness
What You Need:

- A white candle
- A piece of rose quartz

Steps:

1. **Light the Candle:** Light the white candle and hold the rose quartz in your hands.
2. **Speak Forgiveness:** Speak words of forgiveness, such as, "I release anger and invite peace into my heart."
3. **Visualize:** Visualize the relationship healing and growing stronger.

107. Harmony Tea Ritual
What You Need:

- Rose petals
- Lavender
- Chamomile tea

Steps:

1. **Brew the Tea:** Brew a pot of chamomile tea, adding rose petals and lavender for harmony.
2. **Sip Together:** Share this tea with your loved one, focusing on the warmth and love between you.

108. Bonding Bracelet Spell
What You Need:

- Two pieces of pink thread

- A small charm (heart, flower, etc.)

Steps:

1. **Braid the Threads:** Braid the two pieces of thread together, visualizing the bond between you.
2. **Add the Charm:** Tie the charm into the braid.
3. **Wear It:** Both individuals should wear their bracelet to symbolize their unity.

109. Lovers' Knot Ritual
What You Need:

- A red ribbon
- Two candles (one for each person)

Steps:

1. **Tie the Ribbon:** While focusing on the relationship, tie a knot in the ribbon, saying, "May this bond strengthen our love."
2. **Place Between Candles:** Place the ribbon between the candles and light them, letting the warmth symbolize your connection.

110-150. Additional Relationship Harmony Spells
Here are brief overviews of more harmony spells tailored for strengthening relationships during Samhain:

110. Rose Quartz Harmony Jar – Place rose quartz, rosemary, and lavender in a jar; seal it with a pink candle to promote peace.

111. Bonding Seed Ritual – Plant seeds together while focusing on growing your bond.

112. Lovers' Moon Bath – Share a bath infused with rose petals and lavender under the moonlight for emotional bonding.

113. Unity Crystal Grid – Create a crystal grid with rose quartz and amethyst to promote unity in the relationship.

114. Sage and Rose Cleansing – Cleanse your shared space with sage, followed by sprinkling rose petals for love and harmony.

115. Forgiveness Candle – Carve the word "forgiveness" into a white candle and light it to release grudges.

116. Heartfelt Knot Spell – Tie knots in a pink ribbon, each representing a memory or feeling of love and unity.

117. Sunflower Seed Bond – Carry a sunflower seed charm to symbolize a bright, growing relationship.

118. Rose Water Anointing – Anoint each other's wrists with rose water, saying, "I cherish and honor our bond."

119. Samhain Love Knot – Create a love knot with red thread and keep it under your pillow.

120. Autumn Wind Release – On a windy day, write down relationship fears on leaves, releasing them into the wind.

121. Harvesting Love Ritual – Collect apples together and share them, focusing on the harvest of your love.

122. Heartwarming Stone – Carry a piece of carnelian to encourage open-hearted conversations.

123. Harmony Candle – Light a pink candle daily, reciting a blessing for peace in your relationship.

124. Lovers' Mirror Reflection – Sit together and gaze into a mirror, speaking affirmations of unity.

125. Autumn Heart Ritual – Carve a small heart into a pumpkin, fill it with rose petals, and seal it with wax.

126. Samhain Unity Tea – Brew tea with chamomile and rose petals, sharing it to deepen your emotional connection.

127. Bonding Necklace – Wear matching crystal necklaces to symbolize your relationship.

128. Lovers' Sigil – Create a sigil representing your relationship's harmony; draw it on a shared object.

129. Full Moon Gratitude – Under a full moon, express gratitude for each other, strengthening your bond.

130. Heart Knot Bracelet – Braid a bracelet together with pink thread, tying a knot for each cherished memory.

131. Samhain Heart Gem – Exchange rose quartz stones, carrying them as symbols of your love.

132. Lovers' Talisman – Create a charm bag with rosemary and rose petals, placing it in a shared space.

133. The Embrace Candle – Carve your initials into a candle, lighting it to affirm your unity.

134. Forgiveness Jar – Write down grievances, place them in a jar, and bury it to release and forgive.

135. Rose Petal Spell – Scatter rose petals in your home, infusing the space with love and harmony.

136. Binding Ribbon Spell – Wrap a pink ribbon around a small stone, representing your relationship's strength.

137. Moonlit Heart Ritual – Meditate under the moonlight, holding hands, visualizing your love growing stronger.

138. Sunflower Candle – Burn a sunflower-scented candle to invoke joy and lightness in your relationship.

139. Autumn Leaf Bond – Write your names on an autumn leaf, bury it together as a symbol of your lasting bond.

140. Lovers' Embrace Oil – Mix lavender and rose oils, anoint each other's hearts, saying, "I honor our love."

141. Heart-Center Meditation – Meditate together, holding rose quartz, focusing on the love within your hearts.

142. Lovers' Circle – Draw a circle with rose petals, standing within it, holding hands to strengthen your bond.

143. Autumn Reconciliation Tea – Share tea made with chamomile and rose petals, discussing your relationship openly.

144. Knot of Unity – Tie a knot in a pink ribbon for each hope you have for your relationship.

145. Lovers' Lantern – Carve a pumpkin, place a candle inside, lighting it for mutual understanding and unity.

146. Shared Flame Spell – Light a candle together, letting its flame represent your unified energy.

147. Heart-Cleansing Bath – Share a bath infused with lavender and sea salt to cleanse your bond of negativity.

148. Unity Crystal – Place a rose quartz in a shared space, visualizing it radiating harmony.

149. Candlelit Promise – Light a candle and make a promise to each other, sealing it with a kiss.

150. Lovers' Embrace Knot – Tie a knot in a red ribbon, carrying it as a reminder of your commitment.

These relationship harmony spells are designed to nurture the bonds between you and your loved ones, using the magic of Samhain to promote understanding, forgiveness, and unity. Whether you wish to soothe an argument, deepen your connection, or simply reaffirm your love, these rituals can help create an atmosphere of peace and harmony in your relationships.

Chapter 9: Passion and Desire Spells (151-200): Spells to Ignite Passion

Samhain is known as a time of deep, transformative magic, when the veil between the physical and spiritual worlds is at its thinnest. This season is not only about connecting with spirits or reflecting on the past but also about embracing the fire within—reigniting passion, desire, and sensuality in relationships. The spells in this chapter are designed to stoke the flames of passion, using the powerful energies of Samhain to awaken and enhance desire.

These spells incorporate elements of autumn, such as pumpkins, spices, candles, and the mystical energy of the season to bring warmth, excitement, and intimacy to your love life. From simple rituals to more elaborate ceremonies, each spell is crafted to tap into the essence of passion. We begin with the featured spells, "Fire of Desire" and "Pumpkin Spice Passion," and continue with additional rituals to suit various needs and intentions.

151. Fire of Desire

This spell uses the element of fire to awaken and amplify desire, utilizing the warmth and intensity of candles, spices, and intention.

What You Need:

- A red candle (symbolizing passion and desire)
- Cinnamon powder (to heat up passion)
- A small piece of paper and a red pen
- A pinch of cayenne pepper (to intensify desire)

Steps:

1. **Create Your Space:** Set up your altar or workspace with the candle and other ingredients. Cleanse the area with sage or incense to prepare for the ritual.
2. **Write Your Desire:** On the piece of paper, write down your intentions for this spell. Describe the passion you wish to ignite—whether it's rekindling desire in an existing relationship or awakening your own sensual energy.
3. **Anoint the Candle:** Rub a bit of cinnamon powder onto the red candle, saying, "With this spice, I call forth the fire of passion and desire."

4. **Light the Candle:** Light the candle, focusing on its flame. Visualize the flame growing stronger, representing the passion you are igniting.
5. **Burn the Paper:** Sprinkle a pinch of cayenne pepper onto the paper and carefully hold it over the candle flame until it catches fire. Place it in a fireproof dish to burn completely. As it burns, say, "By the fire's light, I ignite the flames of desire. Passion shall burn within me (or us) bright and true."
6. **Close the Ritual:** Allow the candle to burn for a while, then extinguish it safely. Keep the candle for future use in passion-related spells if desired.

152. Pumpkin Spice Passion

This spell incorporates the autumnal symbol of the pumpkin, along with warming spices, to create a magical charm that ignites passion and desire.

What You Need:

- A small pumpkin
- A pinch of cinnamon, nutmeg, and cloves (for warming and passion)
- Honey (to sweeten the passion)
- A red ribbon

Steps:

1. **Prepare the Pumpkin:** Carve a small opening in the top of the pumpkin and scoop out the seeds. As you do this, visualize clearing away any blocks to passion in your life or relationship.
2. **Add Spices and Honey:** Mix the cinnamon, nutmeg, and cloves together with a drop of honey. Place this mixture inside the pumpkin, saying, "By the spices of autumn, I awaken the fire of passion."
3. **Seal with Intention:** Place the lid back on the pumpkin and tie the red ribbon around it, focusing on your desire for warmth, passion, and intimacy. As you tie the ribbon, say, "Bound by this ribbon, passion shall flow and desire shall grow."

4. **Keep the Pumpkin:** Place the pumpkin on your altar or in a shared space to let its energy permeate your environment, infusing it with warmth and passion.

153. Candle of Sensuality
What You Need:

- A red or orange candle
- Cinnamon oil
- A pinch of sugar

Steps:

1. **Anoint the Candle:** Rub cinnamon oil on the candle, focusing on your intention to ignite passion.
2. **Sprinkle Sugar:** Sprinkle a bit of sugar on the candle, saying, "Sweetness and heat, may passion complete."
3. **Light the Candle:** Light the candle and gaze into its flame, visualizing a wave of desire washing over you or your relationship.

154. Lovers' Apple Fire Spell
What You Need:

- A red apple
- A red candle
- A cinnamon stick

Steps:

1. **Carve the Apple:** Carve the initials of you and your lover into the apple.

2. **Light the Candle:** Light the candle and hold the apple close, saying, "By this apple's fire, may passion never tire."
3. **Wrap the Cinnamon Stick:** Wrap the cinnamon stick around the apple with a piece of red ribbon, sealing the spell.

155. Sensual Bath Ritual
What You Need:

- Rose petals
- Cinnamon sticks
- A few drops of ylang-ylang oil

Steps:

1. **Draw the Bath:** Fill the tub with warm water and add rose petals, cinnamon sticks, and ylang-ylang oil.
2. **Soak:** Soak in the bath, focusing on awakening your sensual energy and embracing your body.
3. **Affirm:** As you relax, repeat, "I am a vessel of desire and passion."

156. Autumn Spice Sachet
What You Need:

- A small red pouch
- Cinnamon, nutmeg, and cloves
- A piece of red jasper

Steps:

1. **Fill the Pouch:** Place the spices and the red jasper into the pouch.
2. **Tie with Intention:** Tie the pouch closed, saying, "Spices of autumn, ignite my passion."

3. **Keep the Pouch:** Carry it with you or place it under your pillow to enhance desire.

157. Passion Fruit Ritual
What You Need:

- A pomegranate
- A red candle

Steps:

1. **Light the Candle:** Light the candle and place the pomegranate in front of you.
2. **Speak Your Desire:** While holding the pomegranate, speak your intention to awaken passion.
3. **Eat the Seeds:** Eat the pomegranate seeds, feeling the energy of desire flowing into you.

158. Lovers' Knot Ritual
What You Need:

- A red ribbon
- Rose petals

Steps:

1. **Tie the Knot:** Tie three knots in the ribbon, focusing on the bond of passion between you and your lover.
2. **Place with Rose Petals:** Place the ribbon with rose petals under your pillow.

159. Samhain Spice Candle
What You Need:

- An orange candle
- Cinnamon oil
- Clove powder

Steps:

1. **Anoint the Candle:** Rub cinnamon oil on the candle and sprinkle clove powder.
2. **Light and Visualize:** Light the candle, visualizing your passions being rekindled.

160. Lover's Moon Spell
What You Need:

- A small mirror
- A red candle
- A piece of paper

Steps:

1. **Write Your Desire:** Write your desire for passion on the piece of paper.
2. **Light the Candle:** Place the candle in front of the mirror, light it, and gaze into the mirror's reflection while holding the paper.
3. **Burn the Paper:** Burn the paper in the candle flame, releasing your intention.

161-200. Additional Passion and Desire Spells
Here are brief overviews of more passion spells tailored to Samhain's energy:

161. Apple of Passion – Carve a heart into an apple, rub it with cinnamon, and bury it under the full moon to ignite passion.

162. Fire and Spice Sachet – Fill a sachet with cinnamon, cloves, and nutmeg; carry it with you to boost your sensual energy.

163. Rose Petal Charm – Wrap rose petals in a red ribbon, carry it with you to stir passion within.

164. Lovers' Candle – Carve initials into a red candle, anoint it with cinnamon oil, and light it to strengthen passion.

165. Cinnamon Kiss Spell – Dab cinnamon oil on your lips before kissing your lover to ignite desire.

166. Lovers' Knot Charm – Tie nine knots in a red ribbon, visualizing your bond growing hotter with each knot.

167. Passionate Apple Ritual – Carve your names into an apple, bury it in your garden to grow desire.

168. Lovers' Tea – Brew a tea with cinnamon, rose petals, and honey, drink together to enhance passion.

169. Honey Kiss Ritual – Share a spoonful of honey with your lover, focusing on sweet, passionate love.

170. Autumn Embrace Candle – Light a candle, embrace your partner, and affirm your shared passion.

171. Clove-Infused Spell – Wear a clove in your pocket, charging it with desire energy.

172. Pumpkin Spice Knot – Tie a knot with a red ribbon, sprinkle with pumpkin spice to bind passion.

173. Lover's Flame Ritual – Light two red candles, bring them close together to symbolize your burning passion.

174. Heart-Knot Charm – Tie a heart knot in a red ribbon, carry it to stir passion.

175. Full Moon Desire – Under the full moon, hold a red crystal, visualizing your passion growing.

176. Cinnamon and Rose Bath – Share a bath infused with cinnamon sticks and rose petals to stir sensuality.

177. Lovers' Mirror Spell – Look into a mirror with your lover, visualize your desire amplifying.

178. Warming Spice Jar – Fill a jar with cinnamon, cloves, and nutmeg; seal it with a candle to draw in warmth and passion.

179. Heartbeat Meditation – Meditate with your lover, focusing on synchronizing your heartbeats to enhance intimacy.

180. Lovers' Knot Ritual – Tie nine knots in a ribbon, each representing a wish for passion.

181. Lover's Quartz Charm – Place a rose quartz under your pillow to ignite desire in dreams.

182. Spicy Tea Spell – Brew a tea with cinnamon and cloves, drink together to kindle passion.

183. Lovers' Cauldron – Stir cinnamon and nutmeg in a cauldron, visualize your passion rising.

184. Passion Seed Planting – Plant seeds with your lover, nurturing them to symbolize growing passion.

185. Rose and Clove Charm – Wrap rose petals and cloves in red fabric, place under your bed.

186. Moonlit Kiss Spell – Under the moon, kiss your lover, affirming your passion for each other.

187. Red Ribbon Bond – Tie a ribbon around your wrists together, bind your passion.

188. Lovers' Candle Spell – Light two red candles, let them burn together to unite your passion.

189. Heart-Center Massage – Anoint your lover's chest with rose oil, focusing on warmth and intimacy.

190. Spice-Infused Oil – Mix cinnamon oil, massage each other to ignite sensuality.

191. Lovers' Circle – Create a circle with red candles, sit inside with your lover to meditate on passion.

192. Passion Rose Charm – Wrap rose petals in red fabric, carry it to attract desire.

193. Autumn Fire Ritual – Burn leaves together, releasing any blocks to your passion.

194. Samhain Heart Spell – Carve a heart into a pumpkin, fill with cinnamon, place on altar.

195. Honey Moon Bath – Share a bath with honey and rose petals under the moon.

196. Lovers' Moon Gazing – Gaze at the moon together, focusing on your desire.

197. Lovers' Night Spell – Hold hands, speak desires under the stars.

198. Apple Blossom Tea – Brew apple blossom tea, drink with intention of kindling passion.

199. Samhain Spice Circle – Cast a circle with cinnamon, sit with your lover inside, igniting passion.

200. Heart of Flame – Light a candle, hold hands, speak affirmations of your fiery passion.

These passion and desire spells align with the warmth and intensity of the Samhain season, designed to awaken sensuality, deepen intimacy, and rekindle the flames of love. Whether performed alone or with a partner, these rituals will help you embrace your inner fire, stoking the embers of passion into a glowing flame.

Part II: Luck and Prosperity Spells (201-400)

Chapter 10: General Luck Spells (201-250): Spells to Increase Overall Luck

Samhain, a time of powerful transformative energy and spiritual alignment, is not only about connecting with the spiritual realm but also about manifesting positive outcomes in various aspects of life. Luck spells performed during this magical season harness the abundant energies of autumn, the thinning veil between worlds, and the mysteries of the season. In this chapter, you will find spells designed to increase overall luck, bringing fortune, success, and positivity into your life. From simple charms to more involved rituals, these spells are crafted to shift the energies around you and attract good fortune.

This chapter includes 50 spells, including signature spells like "Jack-o'-Lantern Fortune" and "Good Luck Candle Spell." These rituals use Samhain symbols such as pumpkins, candles, herbs, and spices to invite luck into your life.

201. Jack-o'-Lantern Fortune

The "Jack-o'-Lantern Fortune" spell uses the pumpkin's symbolic power and the protective energy of the jack-o'-lantern to attract luck and fortune into your life.

What You Need:

- A small pumpkin
- A carving knife
- A green candle (representing luck and prosperity)
- A piece of paper and pen
- Cinnamon powder (to attract positive energy)

Steps:

1. **Prepare the Pumpkin:** Carve a jack-o'-lantern face into the pumpkin. As you carve, focus on removing any blocks to luck and opening the door to new opportunities.

2. **Write Your Wish:** On the piece of paper, write down your wish for luck. Fold the paper and sprinkle it with a pinch of cinnamon, saying, "As this cinnamon is sweet, may luck come to me."

3. **Place the Wish Inside:** Place the paper inside the pumpkin. Light the green candle and drip a few drops of wax into the pumpkin to seal your intention.

4. **Illuminate the Pumpkin:** Light the candle and place it inside the pumpkin. Say, "Jack-o'-lantern, light the way, bring me luck by night and day."

5. **Keep the Pumpkin:** Place the pumpkin on your doorstep or in a prominent place in your home. Allow it to radiate luck and good fortune throughout the season.

202. Good Luck Candle Spell

This spell uses the power of a green candle and herbs to invite good fortune into your life. It's a simple but powerful ritual that can be done during the waxing moon or on the night of Samhain.

What You Need:

- A green candle (symbolizing luck and abundance)
- Basil (for prosperity)
- A pinch of salt (for purification)
- A small piece of paper and pen

Steps:

1. **Prepare Your Space:** Cleanse your space by burning sage or incense to clear away any negative energy. Set up your altar with the candle, basil, and salt.

2. **Write Your Intention:** On the paper, write down your intention for luck and prosperity. Be specific about the areas in which you wish to invite good fortune.

3. **Anoint the Candle:** Sprinkle a pinch of salt and basil onto the candle, rubbing it gently into the wax. As you do this, say, "By earth and flame, I call good fortune in my name."

4. **Light the Candle:** Light the green candle and focus on the flame, visualizing it drawing luck toward you like a magnet.

5. **Speak Your Intention:** Hold the piece of paper and say aloud, "As this candle burns, so shall luck come to me, filling my life with fortune and prosperity."
6. **Burn the Paper:** Carefully burn the paper in the candle flame, allowing the ashes to fall into a fireproof dish. Let the candle burn out on its own if possible.

203. Autumn Leaf Luck Charm
What You Need:

- A vibrant autumn leaf
- A small green ribbon
- A pinch of nutmeg (for luck)

Steps:

1. **Hold the Leaf:** Hold the leaf in your hands, focusing on your desire for luck.
2. **Sprinkle Nutmeg:** Sprinkle a pinch of nutmeg onto the leaf, saying, "By autumn's gift, luck shall lift."
3. **Wrap with Ribbon:** Wrap the leaf with the green ribbon to create a small charm. Keep it in your wallet or purse to attract good fortune.

204. Samhain Fortune Jar
What You Need:

- A small jar
- A green candle
- Bay leaves (for success)
- A small coin (for financial luck)
- Cinnamon sticks

Steps:

1. **Fill the Jar:** Place the bay leaves, coin, and cinnamon sticks into the jar, saying, "Fortune flow, prosperity grow."
2. **Seal with Wax:** Light the green candle and allow a few drops of wax to seal the jar.
3. **Place the Jar:** Place the jar in a prominent place in your home to attract luck and fortune.

205. Lucky Apple Ritual
What You Need:

- A red apple
- Honey
- A piece of green paper

Steps:

1. **Carve the Apple:** Carve a small hole in the top of the apple.
2. **Write Your Wish:** On the paper, write down your wish for luck. Fold the paper and place it inside the apple.
3. **Add Honey:** Pour a few drops of honey into the apple, saying, "Sweetness and luck shall flow my way."

206. Pinecone Prosperity Spell
What You Need:

- A pinecone
- Gold or green paint
- A pinch of salt

Steps:

1. **Paint the Pinecone:** Paint the pinecone with gold or green paint, representing wealth and luck.
2. **Sprinkle Salt:** Sprinkle a pinch of salt onto the pinecone, saying, "Protected and prosperous, luck shall surround."
3. **Place the Pinecone:** Place the pinecone on your altar or in your home to attract luck.

207. Candle of Fortune
What You Need:

- A gold candle
- Cinnamon oil

Steps:

1. **Anoint the Candle:** Rub the candle with cinnamon oil, focusing on your desire for luck.
2. **Light the Candle:** Light the candle and visualize luck coming into your life, filling every aspect of your being.

208. Basil Luck Pouch
What You Need:

- A small green pouch
- Basil leaves
- A silver coin

Steps:

1. **Fill the Pouch:** Place the basil leaves and silver coin into the pouch, saying, "Basil and silver, bring luck ever nearer."
2. **Carry the Pouch:** Keep this pouch in your bag or pocket to attract luck wherever you go.

209. Autumn Wind Luck Spell
What You Need:

- A piece of paper
- A pen
- An autumn leaf

Steps:

1. **Write Your Intention:** Write down your wish for luck on the paper.
2. **Wrap with the Leaf:** Wrap the paper around the leaf and hold it up to the wind, saying, "Autumn wind, carry luck to me."

210. Samhain Luck Knot
What You Need:

- A piece of green ribbon

Steps:

1. **Tie Nine Knots:** Tie nine knots in the ribbon, focusing on your intention for luck with each knot.
2. **Keep the Ribbon:** Carry the ribbon with you to draw luck into your life.

211-250. Additional Luck Spells

Here are brief overviews of more general luck spells using the magic of Samhain:

211. Luck Apple Spell – Carve your initials into an apple, rub it with honey, and place it on your altar.

212. Cinnamon Stick Charm – Wrap a cinnamon stick in green fabric, keep it in your wallet for luck.

213. Bay Leaf Wish – Write a wish on a bay leaf, burn it in a candle flame to release the intention.

214. Fortune Pumpkin Seed – Carry a pumpkin seed for good luck during the Samhain season.

215. Lucky Herb Jar – Fill a small jar with basil, rosemary, and sage; seal it with green wax for luck.

216. Good Luck Bath – Add sea salt, basil, and mint to your bath to cleanse and attract good fortune.

217. Lucky Moon Water – Place a jar of water under the moon to charge it with luck.

218. Leaf of Luck – Write your name on an autumn leaf, bury it in the garden to plant your luck.

219. Samhain Fortune Circle – Cast a circle of salt, stand within it, and visualize yourself surrounded by luck.

220. Apple and Clover Charm – Place an apple slice and a clover in a charm bag, carry it with you for luck.

221. Lucky Candle Ring – Place a ring around a lit green candle, visualizing luck entering your life.

222. Samhain Wind Ritual – Speak your wish to the autumn wind, asking it to bring you fortune.

223. Sunflower Seed Spell – Plant sunflower seeds, nurturing them as symbols of growing luck.

224. Clover Knot – Tie a clover into a knot, carry it for luck.

225. Lucky Oil Anointing – Mix cinnamon oil with mint, anoint your wrists to attract luck.

226. Gold Leaf Luck Spell – Paint a leaf gold, place it on your altar as a symbol of abundance.

227. Acorn Luck Charm – Carry an acorn in your pocket for strength and luck.

228. Fortune Stone – Charge a piece of jade under the moon for luck, keep it in your bag.

229. Lucky Incense – Burn cinnamon and sage incense to attract fortune.

230. Good Luck Feather – Find a feather on Samhain, keep it as a talisman for luck.

231. Moonlit Coin Ritual – Place a coin under the moonlight to charge it with luck.

232. Seed of Prosperity – Plant a seed, focusing on it growing as your luck flourishes.

233. Lucky Ring Spell – Place a ring in a dish of salt, leave it overnight to cleanse and attract luck.

234. Autumn Luck Anointing – Anoint your third eye with cinnamon oil to attract good fortune.

235. Jack-o'-Lantern Light – Light a jack-o'-lantern, focusing on its light bringing luck into your home.

236. Sage and Salt Circle – Create a circle with sage and salt, stand within it to draw in luck.

237. Pumpkin Spice Sachet – Fill a sachet with pumpkin spice and carry it for luck.

238. Samhain Wish Jar – Place your wish in a jar with basil and sage, seal it with green wax.

239. Lucky Tea – Brew a tea with basil and mint, drink it while visualizing luck entering your life.

240. Candle of Fortune – Carve your initials into a green candle, light it to manifest luck.

241. Apple Blossom Ritual – Gather apple blossoms, place them under your pillow for sweet dreams and luck.

242. Four-Leaf Clover Spell – Place a clover in your shoe for good fortune.

243. Autumn Seed Spell – Place seeds on your altar, bless them to grow your luck.

244. Fortune Pebble – Find a small pebble, hold it while speaking your wish for luck.

245. Pumpkin Spice Bath – Add pumpkin spice to your bath to cleanse and attract fortune.

246. Moon Water Anointing – Use moon-charged water to anoint your hands before a big task to bring luck.

247. Sage Cleansing – Cleanse your home with sage, inviting luck and positivity.

248. Golden Candle Spell – Light a gold candle, say, "Fortune, flow to me, as the golden light shines free."

249. Samhain Fortune Tea – Brew a tea with cinnamon and clove, drink it to attract luck.

250. Luck Knotting – Tie nine knots in a green ribbon, focusing on luck, carry it with you.

These luck spells use the energy of Samhain to draw good fortune, success, and positivity into your life. Whether you seek to boost your luck for a specific purpose or simply wish to bring more abundance and joy into your daily existence, these rituals align with the season's transformative and abundant energy. May fortune favor you as you work with these spells!

Chapter 11: Money and Abundance Spells (251-300): Spells to Attract Financial Prosperity

Samhain is a time when nature transitions, marking the end of the harvest and the beginning of a new cycle. This potent period of change and transformation can also be harnessed to manifest financial prosperity and abundance. The spells in this chapter are designed to draw wealth, attract monetary opportunities, and encourage financial growth by aligning with the energies of the season.

Incorporating symbols of abundance such as pumpkins, gold, coins, herbs, and spices, these rituals channel the essence of prosperity that Samhain represents. This chapter includes 50 spells, starting with featured spells like the "Cauldron of Wealth" and "Golden Harvest Spell," each crafted to help you manifest your desires for financial security and abundance.

251. Cauldron of Wealth

The "Cauldron of Wealth" spell uses the cauldron's powerful symbolism as a vessel of creation and transformation to draw prosperity into your life.

What You Need:

- A small cauldron or fireproof bowl
- Bay leaves (for prosperity)
- A green candle (symbolizing wealth)
- A coin (preferably gold or silver)
- Cinnamon powder
- A piece of paper and a pen

Steps:

1. **Set Up Your Space:** Cleanse your ritual space with sage or incense. Place the cauldron, candle, bay leaves, coin, and cinnamon on your altar.

2. **Write Your Intention:** On the piece of paper, write down your intention for financial abundance. Be specific about the prosperity you wish to attract, whether it's a new job, increased income, or financial security.
3. **Add the Ingredients:** Place the bay leaves and the coin into the cauldron. Sprinkle a pinch of cinnamon powder over them, saying, "Cinnamon spice, wealth shall grow, abundance flows where this energy goes."
4. **Light the Candle:** Light the green candle and hold it over the cauldron, allowing a few drops of wax to fall into the cauldron, sealing your intention.
5. **Burn the Paper:** Fold the paper with your written intention and light it using the candle flame. Carefully place the burning paper into the cauldron, watching it burn to release your intention into the universe.
6. **Visualize:** As the paper burns, visualize golden light filling the cauldron, expanding outward to envelop you, attracting wealth and abundance into your life.
7. **Close the Ritual:** Allow the candle to burn out on its own if possible. Keep the coin in your wallet or in a place where you handle money as a talisman of ongoing wealth.

252. Golden Harvest Spell

This spell celebrates the energy of harvest and abundance, using seasonal symbols to attract financial prosperity and material wealth.

What You Need:

- A small pumpkin or gourd (representing abundance)
- A gold candle
- A piece of green fabric
- A few coins
- Bay leaves
- Cinnamon stick

Steps:

1. **Prepare the Pumpkin:** Cleanse the pumpkin by wiping it with saltwater to remove any negative energy. As you do this, focus on its symbolic role as a vessel of prosperity.
2. **Create the Abundance Pouch:** On the green fabric, place the coins, bay leaves, and cinnamon stick. Fold the fabric into a small pouch and tie it securely.
3. **Place the Pouch:** Carve a small opening in the pumpkin and place the abundance pouch inside it. Seal the opening with melted wax from the gold candle, saying, "Golden harvest, prosperity grow, abundance and wealth shall always flow."
4. **Light the Candle:** Place the candle next to the pumpkin and light it, focusing on the flame and envisioning your life filled with financial prosperity and wealth.
5. **Keep the Pumpkin:** Place the pumpkin on your altar or in your home as a symbol of abundance for the season. Let it radiate its prosperity energy throughout your space.

253. Coin Bath Ritual
What You Need:

- A green candle
- A handful of coins
- A pinch of sea salt
- A small bowl of water

Steps:

1. **Cleanse the Coins:** Add sea salt to the bowl of water and place the coins inside, saying, "By water and salt, I cleanse these coins to attract prosperity."
2. **Light the Candle:** Light the green candle and focus on your intention for wealth.
3. **Visualize Abundance:** Hold the bowl and visualize it filling with golden light. Leave the bowl on your altar until the candle burns out.

254. Money Attraction Pouch
What You Need:

- A small green pouch
- A piece of jade or green aventurine (for prosperity)
- Basil and mint leaves
- A small coin

Steps:

1. **Fill the Pouch:** Place the stone, herbs, and coin into the pouch, saying, "Jade and herbs, attract wealth to me, as I carry you, abundance flows free."
2. **Carry the Pouch:** Keep the pouch in your pocket, purse, or near your work area to attract financial opportunities.

255. Green Candle Wealth Spell
What You Need:

- A green candle
- A drop of basil oil
- Cinnamon powder

Steps:

1. **Anoint the Candle:** Anoint the candle with basil oil and sprinkle a pinch of cinnamon onto it, focusing on your intention for financial prosperity.
2. **Light the Candle:** Light the candle and visualize money flowing into your life.
3. **Speak Your Intention:** Say, "As this candle burns bright, wealth and prosperity come into sight."

256. Pumpkin Seed Wealth Charm
What You Need:

- A handful of pumpkin seeds
- A small green bag
- A pinch of salt

Steps:

1. **Cleanse the Seeds:** Sprinkle salt over the pumpkin seeds, saying, "Seeds of abundance, cleansed and pure, bring me wealth that's steady and sure."
2. **Fill the Bag:** Place the seeds into the green bag and carry it with you to attract financial prosperity.

257. Harvest Moon Coin Ritual
What You Need:

- A silver or gold coin
- A bowl of water
- A bay leaf

Steps:

1. **Place the Coin:** Place the coin in the bowl of water and set it outside under the light of the moon.
2. **Add the Bay Leaf:** Place the bay leaf in the bowl, saying, "Harvest moon, bring wealth to me, as I will, so shall it be."
3. **Retrieve the Coin:** In the morning, retrieve the coin and keep it in your wallet for continued abundance.

258. Herb-Infused Money Spell

What You Need:

- Basil, mint, and rosemary (for prosperity)
- A green candle
- A piece of paper

Steps:

1. **Light the Candle:** Light the green candle and sprinkle the herbs around it.
2. **Write Your Intention:** Write your financial wish on the paper and place it under the candle.
3. **Burn the Herbs:** Sprinkle some of the herbs into the candle flame, releasing your intention into the universe.

259. Apple Blossom Prosperity Ritual

What You Need:

- A green apple
- Cinnamon powder
- A coin

Steps:

1. **Carve the Apple:** Carve a small hole in the apple and place the coin inside.
2. **Sprinkle Cinnamon:** Sprinkle cinnamon over the apple, saying, "Apple of green, bring wealth unseen."
3. **Bury the Apple:** Bury the apple in your garden to manifest financial growth.

260. Samhain Money Magnet
What You Need:

- A small magnet
- A pinch of nutmeg (for luck)
- A green ribbon

Steps:

1. **Wrap the Magnet:** Sprinkle nutmeg onto the magnet and wrap it with the green ribbon.
2. **Speak Your Intention:** Say, "Magnet of luck, draw wealth to me, abundance flows, as I decree."
3. **Keep the Magnet:** Place the magnet near your workspace or in your wallet to attract financial success.

261-300. Additional Money and Abundance Spells
Here are brief overviews of additional money spells tailored to Samhain's energy:

261. Bay Leaf Wealth Charm – Write "Wealth" on a bay leaf and place it in your wallet.

262. Pumpkin Prosperity Spell – Carve your initials into a pumpkin, anoint it with cinnamon oil, and place it on your altar.

263. Green Candle Knotting – Tie nine knots in a green ribbon while focusing on financial prosperity.

264. Abundance Bath – Add basil, mint, and sea salt to your bath to cleanse and attract wealth.

265. Prosperity Jar – Fill a jar with basil, bay leaves, and coins; seal it with green wax.

266. Moonlit Coin Ritual – Charge a coin under the full moon and keep it as a prosperity talisman.

267. Golden Seed Spell – Place a gold-painted pumpkin seed in your purse for ongoing wealth.

268. Cinnamon and Mint Anointing – Mix cinnamon and mint oils, anoint your wallet to attract money.

269. Herb Sachet – Fill a sachet with rosemary and bay leaves, place it in your cash drawer to attract money.

270. Golden Apple Ritual – Anoint an apple with cinnamon, place it on your altar to attract financial abundance.

271. Luck Coin Ritual – Hold a coin in your hands, speak your financial wishes into it, and keep it in your wallet.

272. Autumn Leaf Wealth Spell – Write your intention on an autumn leaf, bury it to grow your wealth.

273. Basil Money Charm – Carry basil leaves in a green pouch to attract money.

274. Gold Candle Ritual – Light a gold candle, visualize money flowing into your life.

275. Prosperity Ring Spell – Wear a ring charged with basil oil as a symbol of attracting wealth.

276. Jade Stone Wealth – Keep a jade stone in your workspace to draw financial opportunities.

277. Mint Coin Ritual – Anoint a coin with mint oil, keep it in your pocket for prosperity.

278. Harvest Knot – Tie nine knots in a green ribbon, bury it in your garden for abundance.

279. Clover Money Spell – Find a clover, press it in your wallet to attract money.

280. Pinecone Abundance – Place a pinecone on your altar, visualize it growing wealth in your life.

281. Samhain Money Jar – Fill a jar with coins and herbs, light a green candle beside it to attract wealth.

282. Honey Wealth Spell – Drizzle honey over a coin, bury it to attract sweetness and abundance.

283. Prosperity Seed Planting – Plant seeds with the intention of growing your finances.

284. Basil Oil Anointing – Anoint your hands with basil oil before handling money to attract prosperity.

285. Moonlit Bay Leaf – Place a bay leaf under the moonlight, keep it as a wealth talisman.

286. Apple of Wealth – Carve your name into an apple, place it on your altar for prosperity.

287. Cinnamon Stick Spell – Carry a cinnamon stick wrapped in a green ribbon to attract money.

288. Green Ribbon Ritual – Tie a green ribbon around a candle, light it to attract financial success.

289. Fortune Pumpkin Charm – Fill a small pumpkin with coins and bay leaves, place it near your front door.

290. Clover and Mint – Place a clover and mint in a sachet, keep it in your bag for money luck.

291. Good Fortune Bath – Add rosemary and basil to your bath to cleanse and attract wealth.

292. Golden Seed Ritual – Paint pumpkin seeds gold, carry them as charms for financial abundance.

293. Samhain Money Blessing – Under the moon, hold coins in your hand, visualizing them multiplying.

294. Pinecone Money Magnet – Place a pinecone near your cash register or workspace to attract sales.

295. Cinnamon and Basil Sachet – Fill a sachet with cinnamon and basil, keep it in your cash drawer.

296. Lucky Coin Spell – Place a coin in a bowl of salt under the moonlight, keep it as a money magnet.

297. Harvest Money Jar – Fill a jar with coins and herbs, seal it with a green candle's wax for ongoing wealth.

298. Abundance Knotting – Tie a green ribbon around a coin, bury it to grow financial prosperity.

299. Mint-Infused Wallet – Rub mint leaves inside your wallet to attract money.

300. Wealth Attraction Circle – Cast a circle with coins, stand within it, and visualize wealth flowing into your life.

These money and abundance spells utilize the magic of Samhain to attract financial prosperity and wealth. By incorporating the symbols of the season, such as pumpkins, herbs, and candles, these rituals align with the energy of growth and transformation that Samhain embodies. Use these spells to manifest financial success, security, and abundance in your life.

Chapter 12: Job and Career Spells (301-350): Spells for Job Success and Career Advancement

Samhain is a time of reflection, transformation, and preparation for the future, making it a powerful season to cast spells that focus on job success and career advancement. Whether you're seeking a new job, aiming for a promotion, or wanting to excel in your current role, the spells in this chapter use the energies of autumn to create the conditions for professional growth and success.

These job and career spells leverage symbols of prosperity, growth, strength, and opportunity, using candles, herbs, and seasonal elements to align your career path with the abundance and transformation that Samhain represents. This chapter includes 50 spells, starting with the featured "Samhain Career Boost" and "Witch's Wealth Ladder," followed by additional rituals that cater to various career goals and aspirations.

301. Samhain Career Boost

The "Samhain Career Boost" spell harnesses the power of the season to enhance your career prospects, attract new opportunities, and help you excel in your professional life.

What You Need:

- A green candle (for success and growth)
- A gold coin (symbolizing wealth and career advancement)
- Rosemary and basil (for luck and prosperity)
- A small piece of paper and a pen
- A bowl

Steps:

1. **Prepare Your Space:** Cleanse your workspace or altar by burning sage or rosemary incense. Place the green candle, coin, herbs, and paper on the altar.
2. **Write Your Career Intention:** On the piece of paper, write down your specific career goals. Be detailed about what you wish to achieve, whether it's getting a new job, earning a promotion, or gaining recognition in your field.

3. **Place the Coin:** Place the gold coin in the bowl, sprinkling a pinch of rosemary and basil over it. As you do this, say, "Herbs of luck and success, bring opportunities to me. Career growth and wealth, so mote it be."
4. **Anoint the Candle:** Light the green candle, focusing on your intention for career advancement. Visualize yourself succeeding, achieving your goals, and feeling confident in your career path.
5. **Burn the Paper:** Carefully light the paper with your written intention from the candle flame and place it into the bowl to burn. As the paper burns, visualize your career path opening up and new opportunities manifesting.
6. **Keep the Coin:** Once the spell is complete, keep the coin in your wallet or on your desk as a talisman of ongoing career success.

302. Witch's Wealth Ladder

This spell uses the symbolism of a ladder to represent career progression, allowing you to "climb" toward success and wealth in your professional life.

What You Need:

- A small ladder charm (or create a makeshift ladder using twigs and string)
- Green thread or ribbon
- A small piece of jade or citrine (for career success)
- Cinnamon stick (to attract prosperity)

Steps:

1. **Create the Ladder:** If you don't have a ladder charm, create a small ladder using twigs and the green thread. As you construct the ladder, focus on your desire to ascend in your career.
2. **Add the Stone and Cinnamon:** Tie the piece of jade or citrine and the cinnamon stick to the ladder using the green thread. As you tie each element, say, "With each step, I rise in success, prosperity follows, I am truly blessed."

3. **Place the Ladder:** Place the ladder on your desk or hang it in your workspace to draw career success and financial abundance.
4. **Visualize:** Each time you see the ladder, visualize yourself climbing higher in your career, achieving your professional goals.

303. Samhain Job Opportunity Spell
What You Need:

- A green candle
- A piece of paper
- A key (symbolizing new opportunities)

Steps:

1. **Write Your Intentions:** On the paper, write down the job opportunity you seek.
2. **Light the Candle:** Light the green candle, focusing on opening the door to new job opportunities.
3. **Place the Key:** Hold the key and say, "Key of opportunity, open the door to my dream job."
4. **Keep the Key:** Carry the key with you until the job opportunity manifests.

304. Career Confidence Spell
What You Need:

- A yellow candle (for confidence)
- A piece of carnelian (for courage and motivation)
- A pinch of basil

Steps:

1. **Anoint the Candle:** Rub the yellow candle with basil, focusing on filling yourself with confidence.
2. **Light the Candle:** Light the candle, holding the carnelian in your hands, saying, "Confidence rise, success be mine."
3. **Carry the Stone:** Carry the carnelian with you to boost confidence in your workplace.

305. Green Ribbon Promotion Spell
What You Need:

- A piece of green ribbon
- A gold coin

Steps:

1. **Tie Nine Knots:** As you tie each knot in the green ribbon, focus on different aspects of the promotion you desire.
2. **Wrap the Coin:** Wrap the coin in the ribbon, saying, "Promotion come, success be mine."
3. **Keep the Charm:** Keep this charm in your workspace.

306. Success Charm Bag
What You Need:

- A small green pouch
- Bay leaves
- Rosemary
- A small piece of jade

Steps:

1. **Fill the Pouch:** Place the bay leaves, rosemary, and jade into the pouch.
2. **Speak Your Intention:** Hold the pouch and say, "Success I draw, prosperity flows, my career path brightly glows."
3. **Carry the Pouch:** Carry this charm with you to attract success.

307. Samhain Career Cleansing Spell
What You Need:

- A bowl of water
- Sea salt
- Rosemary

Steps:

1. **Prepare the Water:** Add sea salt and rosemary to the bowl of water.
2. **Wash Your Hands:** Dip your hands into the water, saying, "I cleanse away doubts, my career path clears, success and abundance draw near."

308. Abundance Stone Spell
What You Need:

- A piece of citrine
- A green candle

Steps:

1. **Charge the Stone:** Hold the citrine in your hands and visualize it filling with golden light.

2. **Light the Candle:** Light the candle, saying, "Citrine bright, attract career success and light."
3. **Place the Stone:** Keep the stone on your desk to draw abundance.

309. Harvest Moon Career Boost
What You Need:

- A small bowl of water
- A bay leaf
- A coin

Steps:

1. **Place Under the Moon:** Place the bowl outside under the light of the full moon with the coin and bay leaf inside.
2. **Speak Your Intentions:** Say, "Harvest moon, bring me success, career growth and wealth, I do confess."
3. **Use the Water:** In the morning, use the water to anoint your hands before work.

310. Samhain Success Candle
What You Need:

- A green candle
- A piece of rosemary

Steps:

1. **Anoint the Candle:** Rub the rosemary on the candle, saying, "Success be mine, wealth and career align."
2. **Light the Candle:** Focus on your career goals as the candle burns.

311-350. Additional Job and Career Spells

Here are more job and career spells tailored for Samhain's energy:

311. Bay Leaf Job Spell – Write your career goal on a bay leaf, burn it while focusing on achieving that goal.

312. Career Knotting – Tie nine knots in a green ribbon, each representing a step toward career success.

313. Apple Blossom Success – Place apple blossoms on your desk for prosperity.

314. Job Confidence Oil – Anoint your wrists with rosemary oil before an interview or meeting.

315. Career Growth Stone – Carry a piece of moss agate to symbolize steady growth in your career.

316. Pinecone Prosperity – Place a pinecone on your desk to attract career opportunities.

317. Promotion Candle – Carve your name into a green candle, light it while focusing on your desired promotion.

318. Career Mirror Spell – Look into a mirror, stating affirmations of your career success.

319. Basil Money Charm – Carry a basil leaf in your wallet for financial success at work.

320. Career Success Bath – Add rosemary and mint to your bath for confidence and success.

321. Golden Ladder Spell – Visualize a golden ladder during meditation, each step representing career advancement.

322. Lucky Penny Ritual – Place a penny under your pillow before an interview for good luck.

323. Abundance Tea – Brew a tea with basil and mint, drink it while focusing on career prosperity.

324. Harvest Success Ritual – Hold a handful of grains, visualize your career growing, scatter them outside.

325. Success Incense – Burn cinnamon incense in your workspace to attract success.

326. Career Cleansing Bath – Bathe with sea salt and rosemary to cleanse away work-related negativity.

327. Moonstone Career Spell – Keep a moonstone on your desk to attract new career opportunities.

328. Green Ribbon Knot – Tie a green ribbon around your wrist, focusing on job success with each knot.

329. Job Opportunity Oil – Anoint your resume with mint oil to attract job offers.

330. Job Interview Charm – Carry a piece of citrine in your pocket during interviews for confidence.

331. Fortune Seed Planting – Plant seeds in your garden, focusing on growing your career.

332. Clover Success Charm – Carry a clover in your wallet for good fortune at work.

333. Pine Needle Spell – Place pine needles in a sachet, keep it at your workspace for protection and success.

334. Moonlit Rosemary Ritual – Leave a sprig of rosemary under the moon, keep it in your workspace.

335. Jade Stone Success – Place a jade stone on your desk, focusing on drawing career growth.

336. Samhain Resume Ritual – Before sending out resumes, burn rosemary and wave the smoke over them for luck.

337. Harvest Basket Spell – Create a small basket with grains, herbs, and a coin, place it on your desk.

338. Mint Success Spell – Rub mint leaves on your hands before work to invite success.

339. Apple Fortune – Keep a small apple on your desk for career prosperity.

340. Success Mirror Affirmation – Daily, look into a mirror and speak affirmations of career success.

341. Green Candle Focus – Light a green candle while visualizing your career goals.

342. Success Anointing Oil – Anoint your forehead with basil oil before starting work.

343. Lucky Clover Ritual – Place a four-leaf clover under your desk for ongoing luck.

344. Career Crystal Grid – Arrange citrine and jade in a grid on your desk to attract career opportunities.

345. Pinecone Job Success – Carry a small pinecone for continued success.

346. Clover Leaf Bath – Add clover leaves to your bath before important career events.

347. Rosemary Focus Ritual – Place rosemary on your desk to promote clarity and success.

348. Fortune Moon Spell – Under the full moon, visualize yourself succeeding in your career.

349. Green Ribbon Wealth – Tie a green ribbon around a coin, keep it on your desk.

350. Career Success Circle – Cast a circle with rosemary, sit within it, focusing on career growth.

These job and career spells harness the transformative energy of Samhain to help you achieve your professional goals. By aligning with the season's themes of growth, opportunity, and abundance, these spells empower you to manifest success, gain recognition, and progress in your chosen career path. Use them to enhance your job prospects and build a prosperous future.

Chapter 13: Business Success Spells (351-400): Spells Tailored for Business Owners

Samhain, the time of the final harvest, is an ideal period for business owners to harness the season's transformative energies to ensure growth, prosperity, and success. This chapter focuses on spells specifically tailored for business owners who wish to attract new customers, increase sales, and create a thriving business environment. Utilizing the power of candles, herbs, seasonal symbols, and the abundant energy of autumn, these spells are designed to align your business with financial success and prosperity.

From simple charms to more intricate rituals, these 50 spells are created to help manifest wealth, boost customer attraction, enhance financial stability, and create an atmosphere of success around your business. We begin with signature spells like the "Prosperous Pumpkin Charm" and the "Harvest Sales Spell," followed by a collection of additional spells suited for various business needs.

351. Prosperous Pumpkin Charm

The "Prosperous Pumpkin Charm" draws upon the pumpkin's symbol of abundance and prosperity to bring growth and success to your business.

What You Need:

- A small pumpkin or gourd (representing abundance)
- A green ribbon
- Bay leaves (for success)
- Cinnamon sticks (to attract wealth)
- A small gold coin or piece of pyrite

Steps:

1. **Cleanse the Pumpkin:** Start by cleansing the pumpkin with saltwater or sage smoke to remove any negative energy. Focus on transforming the pumpkin into a vessel of business success.

2. **Prepare the Prosperity Pouch:** Take a small piece of fabric (green, if possible) and place the bay leaves, cinnamon sticks, and gold coin or pyrite inside. Tie it securely with the green ribbon to form a small pouch.
3. **Carve a Small Opening:** Carefully carve a small hole into the pumpkin. Place the prosperity pouch inside, visualizing your business filling with abundance and success.
4. **Seal with Intention:** Close the hole with the pumpkin's stem or by tying another piece of green ribbon around it. As you do this, say, "Prosperous pumpkin, vessel of wealth, bring my business fortune, success, and health."
5. **Place the Pumpkin:** Place the pumpkin near the entrance of your business or in your workspace to attract prosperity. Leave it there throughout the season to allow its energy to permeate your business.

352. Harvest Sales Spell

The "Harvest Sales Spell" uses the energy of the harvest to draw in customers and increase sales, filling your business with abundance.

What You Need:

- A green candle (symbolizing growth and prosperity)
- A piece of paper
- A pen
- A handful of grains (rice, barley, or corn)
- A small bowl

Steps:

1. **Create Your Intention:** On the piece of paper, write down the specific sales goals or customer numbers you wish to achieve. Be as clear and detailed as possible to give your spell a defined target.
2. **Prepare the Bowl:** Place the grains into the bowl, focusing on them as symbols of an abundant harvest.

3. **Light the Candle:** Light the green candle, placing it beside the bowl. Visualize your business thriving with customers and successful sales transactions.
4. **Speak Your Intention:** Hold the paper over the bowl and say, "By the harvest's light and grain's gold, sales grow steady, success take hold."
5. **Place the Paper:** Fold the paper and place it under the bowl. Let the candle burn for a while, absorbing the energy of your intention.
6. **Close the Ritual:** After the candle has burned down safely, keep the bowl of grains in your workspace or store as a symbol of ongoing sales success.

353. Bay Leaf Business Boost
What You Need:

- A handful of bay leaves
- A green ribbon
- A small piece of paper

Steps:

1. **Write Your Intention:** On the piece of paper, write down your business goals or intentions for growth and prosperity.
2. **Wrap with Bay Leaves:** Wrap the paper in bay leaves and secure it with the green ribbon, saying, "Bay leaves of strength, boost my business, bring success to every length."
3. **Keep in Business Space:** Place the bundle in your office or store to draw in success.

354. Business Attraction Sachet
What You Need:

- A small green sachet
- Rosemary (for success)
- Basil (for wealth)

- Mint (to attract customers)

Steps:

1. **Fill the Sachet:** Place the herbs into the sachet, focusing on attracting customers and wealth.
2. **Speak Your Intention:** Say, "Herbs of growth, bring wealth and clients, make my business strong and resilient."
3. **Keep in Your Workspace:** Hang the sachet near your cash register or in your office to attract prosperity.

355. Green Candle Sales Spell
What You Need:

- A green candle
- Basil oil (to attract prosperity)
- A pinch of cinnamon

Steps:

1. **Anoint the Candle:** Anoint the candle with basil oil, then sprinkle cinnamon on it while focusing on your business's success.
2. **Light the Candle:** Light the candle and say, "Green flame bright, bring sales to me, success in business, prosperity set free."
3. **Burn During Business Hours:** Light the candle during business hours to draw customers.

356. Money Bowl Ritual
What You Need:

- A small bowl
- Coins
- Bay leaves
- Cinnamon sticks

Steps:

1. **Fill the Bowl:** Place the coins, bay leaves, and cinnamon sticks into the bowl, saying, "Wealth and fortune, fill this place, bring success at every pace."
2. **Place in Business:** Keep this bowl on your desk or in your store as a magnet for prosperity.

357. Business Success Knot
What You Need:

- A piece of green ribbon
- A small charm (coin, key, etc.)

Steps:

1. **Tie Nine Knots:** As you tie each knot in the ribbon, visualize different aspects of your business success.
2. **Add the Charm:** Attach the charm to the ribbon, saying, "Knots of nine, bring success in line, wealth and fortune, now combine."
3. **Hang in Your Workspace:** Hang this charm in your workspace.

358. New Customer Attraction Spell
What You Need:

- A green candle
- A handful of mint leaves
- A small bowl

Steps:

1. **Place the Mint:** Place the mint leaves in the bowl, saying, "Mint so bright, bring customers near, fill my business with profit and cheer."
2. **Light the Candle:** Light the candle beside the bowl, visualizing new customers walking into your business.

359. Moonlit Business Blessing
What You Need:

- A silver coin
- A small bowl of water
- A bay leaf

Steps:

1. **Place Under the Moon:** Place the bowl of water, the coin, and the bay leaf outside under the light of the moon.
2. **Speak Your Blessing:** Say, "Moon so bright, bless my business this night, bring customers and wealth, in fortune's light."
3. **Keep the Coin:** In the morning, retrieve the coin and keep it near your business cash register.

360. Prosperity Pinecone Spell
What You Need:

- A pinecone
- Gold or green paint
- A piece of ribbon

Steps:

1. **Paint the Pinecone:** Paint the pinecone gold or green, representing wealth and growth.
2. **Tie with Ribbon:** Wrap a ribbon around the pinecone, saying, "Pinecone of growth, fortune arise, bring my business success in size."
3. **Place in Workspace:** Place the pinecone in your workspace.

361-400. Additional Business Success Spells

Here are additional business success spells tailored for Samhain's energy:

361. Cinnamon Stick Charm – Wrap a cinnamon stick in green fabric, place it near your cash register for financial growth.

362. Bay Leaf Success – Write your business name on a bay leaf, burn it in a candle flame while focusing on prosperity.

363. Green Candle Knotting – Tie nine knots in a green ribbon, each knot representing a business goal.

364. Rosemary Sales Spell – Hang rosemary above your store's entrance to attract customers.

365. Basil Infusion – Place basil in a bowl of water near your workspace to draw in prosperity.

366. Golden Seed Ritual – Carry a gold-painted pumpkin seed as a business success charm.

367. Money Anointing Oil – Mix cinnamon and mint oils, anoint your business cards to attract wealth.

368. Harvest Bag – Create a charm bag with grains and herbs, place it in your workspace for abundance.

369. Mint Attracting Spell – Place mint leaves under your business sign to draw in customers.

370. Green Stone Ritual – Place a piece of jade on your desk to attract financial success.

371. Luck Coin – Place a coin in your business's cash register to encourage ongoing prosperity.

372. Pine Needle Charm – Keep a sachet of pine needles in your store to protect and boost business.

373. Clover Sales – Hang a clover in your store to attract customers.

374. Moonstone Business Spell – Place a moonstone under your counter to enhance sales.

375. Lucky Apple Ritual – Place an apple on your desk to symbolize a bountiful business.

376. Cinnamon Stick Wealth – Carry a cinnamon stick wrapped in a green ribbon to attract wealth.

377. Bay Leaf Knot – Tie a bay leaf into a green ribbon, hang it in your workspace.

378. Moonlit Sales – Place a silver coin outside under the moon, keep it in your store.

379. Sunflower Seed Growth – Plant sunflower seeds around your business, focusing on financial growth.

380. Pinecone and Mint – Place a pinecone and mint leaves near your entrance.

381. Apple Blossom Success – Scatter apple blossoms around your business space.

382. Rosemary Cleansing – Use rosemary-infused water to cleanse your business.

383. Fortune Candle – Carve your business's name into a green candle, light it.

384. Abundance Jar – Fill a jar with coins and herbs, seal it with green wax.

385. Seed Planting – Plant seeds with your business goals in mind.

386. Golden Leaf Ritual – Paint a leaf gold, keep it near your workspace.

387. Basil Business Charm – Carry a basil leaf for ongoing success.

388. Mint Anointing – Anoint your store's door with mint oil.

389. Green Candle Wealth – Light a green candle, focusing on financial abundance.

390. Harvest Success – Hold grains, scatter them around your business.

391. Rosemary Circle – Create a circle with rosemary, stand within it.

392. Apple of Wealth – Carve your business name into an apple, place it in your store.

393. Jade and Mint – Place jade and mint near your workspace.

394. Success Grid – Create a crystal grid for wealth.

395. Prosperity Ladder – Visualize a ladder, climbing it towards success.

396. Money Knot – Tie knots in a green ribbon, each representing a financial goal.

397. Clover Leaf – Place a clover leaf under your cash register.

398. Green Ribbon Charm – Tie a green ribbon around a coin.

399. Moonlit Ritual – Under the moon, speak words of prosperity.

400. Circle of Wealth – Cast a circle with coins, stand within it.

These business success spells tap into the energy of Samhain, focusing on attracting customers, increasing sales, and fostering financial stability. By harnessing the symbols of autumn abundance, these spells help manifest a prosperous business environment. May your business thrive and grow with the power of these rituals!

Part III: Protection Spells (401-600)

Chapter 14: Home Protection Spells (401-450): Spells to Safeguard Your Home

Samhain marks the thinning of the veil between the worlds, a time when both positive and negative energies are at their peak. As such, it is an ideal time to strengthen the protective wards around your home. The spells in this chapter focus on safeguarding your space from harmful influences, unwanted energies, and negative spirits. Using the symbolism of autumn, elements from nature, and the power of intention, these spells create a shield of security and peace around your home.

Each of the 50 spells in this chapter, including the featured "Guardian of the Gate" and "Pumpkin Warding Ritual," is designed to invoke protective energies and create a safe haven. Whether you're seeking to repel negativity, protect your family, or maintain a positive atmosphere, these spells will help establish a secure and harmonious environment for you and your loved ones.

401. Guardian of the Gate

The "Guardian of the Gate" spell calls upon protective forces to guard the entrances of your home, ensuring that only positive energies and friendly spirits may enter.

What You Need:

- Two small, protective statues or figurines (such as gargoyles, dragons, or animal guardians)
- A bowl of salt
- A sprig of rosemary (for purification and protection)
- A black candle (for banishing negativity)
- A small dish of water

Steps:

1. **Cleanse Your Space:** Before beginning the spell, cleanse your space by burning rosemary or sage. Focus on clearing away any lingering negative energies.
2. **Prepare the Statues:** Place the two statues near the main entrance of your home. These will act as your "guardians." Pour the salt into the small dish and sprinkle some around the statues, creating a protective boundary.

3. **Light the Candle:** Light the black candle and hold the sprig of rosemary. Close your eyes and visualize a strong, invisible force surrounding your home, creating a barrier that only positive energy can pass through.
4. **Bless the Statues:** Dip your fingers in the dish of water and sprinkle a few drops on each statue while saying, "Guardians of the gate, protect this space. Let no harm nor ill intent cross this threshold. As I will, so mote it be."
5. **Seal with Salt:** Take a pinch of salt from the bowl and sprinkle it at the base of each statue, enhancing the protective barrier.
6. **Keep the Statues:** Leave the statues at your entrance to continually guard and protect your home. You can repeat this spell periodically, especially during Samhain or any time you feel the need for additional protection.

402. Pumpkin Warding Ritual

This spell utilizes the pumpkin's natural protective properties and the energies of the harvest season to ward off negative spirits and shield your home from unwanted influences.

What You Need:

- A small pumpkin
- A carving knife
- Salt
- A black candle
- Rosemary and sage leaves

Steps:

1. **Prepare the Pumpkin:** Carve the top off the pumpkin and scoop out the seeds. As you do this, imagine removing any negative energies from your home.
2. **Fill with Protection:** Place a handful of salt inside the pumpkin, followed by the rosemary and sage leaves. These herbs are known for their protective and purifying qualities.

3. **Carve a Protective Symbol:** Carve a simple protective symbol, such as a pentacle or a rune, into the front of the pumpkin. As you carve, focus on the intention of protection and warding.
4. **Light the Candle:** Place the black candle inside the pumpkin and light it. Visualize the light creating a shield around your home, repelling any negative energies or spirits.
5. **Speak Your Intention:** Say, "Pumpkin of the harvest, ward this place. Keep out ill will and protect this space. With salt and flame, my home is sealed, by this rite, all harm is repealed."
6. **Place the Pumpkin:** Set the pumpkin near your front door or in another prominent area to act as a protective ward. Leave it there throughout the season to maintain its protective energy.

403. Salt Circle Protection
What You Need:

- Sea salt
- A small bowl

Steps:

1. **Create the Circle:** Sprinkle a circle of sea salt around the perimeter of your home, focusing on the intention of protection.
2. **Speak the Spell:** As you walk around your home, say, "Salt of earth, protective force, guard my home from harm's course."
3. **Keep the Salt:** Place a small bowl of salt near each entrance to maintain the protective circle.

404. Doorway Herb Bundle
What You Need:

- A bundle of rosemary, sage, and thyme
- A piece of black ribbon

Steps:

1. **Create the Bundle:** Tie the herbs together with the black ribbon, focusing on the intention of protection.
2. **Hang Above the Door:** Hang the herb bundle above your front door to ward off negative energies.

405. Warding Candle Spell
What You Need:

- A black candle
- Rosemary oil

Steps:

1. **Anoint the Candle:** Rub rosemary oil on the candle, focusing on your intention of creating a protective barrier.
2. **Light the Candle:** Light the candle and say, "Candle of black, guard this place. Warding flame, shield this space."

406. Mirror Protection Spell
What You Need:

- A small mirror
- Black paint or marker

Steps:

1. **Prepare the Mirror:** Paint a protective symbol (such as a pentacle) on the back of the mirror.

2. **Hang Facing Outward:** Place the mirror facing outward near your front door to reflect and repel negative energies.

407. Basil Home Protection
What You Need:

- Fresh basil leaves
- A small bowl of water

Steps:

1. **Cleanse with Basil:** Dip the basil leaves in the water and sprinkle it around the entrances of your home, saying, "Basil of green, guard unseen. Keep my home safe and clean."

408. Iron Nail Warding
What You Need:

- An iron nail

Steps:

1. **Place the Nail:** Place an iron nail above your doorway to ward off negative spirits and energies.

409. Protective Crystal Grid
What You Need:

- Black tourmaline, obsidian, and clear quartz crystals

Steps:

1. **Arrange the Crystals:** Place the crystals around your home, forming a protective grid. Black tourmaline and obsidian repel negativity, while clear quartz amplifies the protective energies.
2. **Speak the Spell:** As you arrange each crystal, say, "Crystals of earth, protect this space, keep it safe with your grace."

410. Protective Moon Water
What You Need:

- A jar of water
- Sea salt
- A piece of black obsidian

Steps:

1. **Prepare the Water:** Add a pinch of sea salt and the obsidian to the jar of water.
2. **Charge Under the Moon:** Place the jar outside under the full moon to charge it with protective energy.
3. **Use the Water:** Sprinkle the moon water around the entrances of your home for protection.

411-450. Additional Home Protection Spells
Here are brief overviews of more home protection spells using the magic of Samhain:

411. Warding Herb Sachet – Create a sachet with rosemary, sage, and bay leaves, hang it by your front door.

412. Pumpkin Seed Shield – Place pumpkin seeds around your home to create a protective barrier.

413. Iron Nail Protection – Bury an iron nail at each corner of your property for a strong protective boundary.

414. Salt and Rosemary Circle – Sprinkle a circle of salt and rosemary around your home, focusing on protection.

415. Protective Wind Chime – Hang a wind chime made of bells and black ribbon to ward off negative spirits.

416. Warding Oil Anointing – Mix rosemary oil with sea salt, anoint doorways and windows for protection.

417. Sunflower Guardian – Plant sunflowers near the entrance to your home to guard against negativity.

418. Pentacle Mirror Spell – Place a pentacle on a mirror facing outward to reflect harm away.

419. Doorstep Salt Spell – Sprinkle salt on your doorstep, saying, "Salt of earth, keep harm away."

420. Bay Leaf Protection – Place bay leaves above doorways and windows to repel negative energies.

421. Warding Candle Circle – Light four black candles, placing them at the four corners of your home for protection.

422. Basil Anointing Oil – Use basil-infused oil to anoint door frames, creating a protective barrier.

423. Doorstep Crystal Spell – Place black tourmaline near your front door to ward off negativity.

424. Hearth Protection Spell – Burn rosemary and sage in your fireplace to cleanse and protect your home.

425. Pinecone Warding – Hang a pinecone near your door to ward off unwanted energies.

426. Saltwater Spray – Mix salt in water, spray it around your home to cleanse and protect.

427. Candle of Light – Burn a white candle near a window to keep away negative spirits.

428. Mirror of Deflection – Place a small mirror in each corner of a room to reflect negativity away.

429. Herb Door Sweep – Sprinkle rosemary and salt across the threshold to prevent negative energies from entering.

430. Black Ribbon Knotting – Tie nine knots in a black ribbon, hang it above your door for protection.

431. Moonlight Protection – Place a jar of water under the moon, sprinkle it around your home.

432. Rosemary Bundle – Hang a bundle of dried rosemary by your entrance for continuous protection.

433. Basil Plant Guardian – Keep a basil plant near your entrance to absorb negative energies.

434. Salt Circle Ritual – Create a salt circle around your home, focusing on warding off negativity.

435. Apple of Protection – Place an apple on your windowsill to guard against harm.

436. Sage Smudging – Smudge your home with sage, focusing on each corner to remove negativity.

437. Pumpkin Seed Protection – Carry pumpkin seeds in a pouch as a charm.

438. Protective Bath – Add sea salt and rosemary to a bath to cleanse and shield yourself.

439. Saltwater Doorstep – Pour saltwater across your doorstep for protection.

440. Candle Flame Shield – Light a black candle near a window to act as a shield.

441. Warding Bell – Hang a small bell by your front door to ward off negativity.

442. Lavender Warding – Place dried lavender under your pillow to keep negative spirits away.

443. Pine Needle Circle – Create a circle with pine needles around your home.

444. Salt Bowl Protection – Place a bowl of salt in each room to absorb negative energies.

445. Iron Horseshoe – Hang an iron horseshoe above your door for good luck and protection.

446. Bay Leaf Anointing – Rub bay leaves on your door frames.

447. Moonstone Warding – Place a moonstone in each room to shield against harmful energies.

448. Protective Sigil – Draw a protective sigil on a piece of paper, place it under your doormat.

449. Sage and Pinecone Charm – Hang a pinecone tied with sage near your window.

450. Samhain Blessing – On Samhain night, light a candle and bless your home.

These home protection spells use the energy of Samhain to create a barrier against negative forces, ensuring your living space remains safe and peaceful. By utilizing elements of autumn and the powerful symbolism of the season, these rituals provide continuous protection throughout the year. May your home be ever-guarded and filled with positive energy.

Chapter 15: Personal Protection Spells (451-500): Spells for Personal Safety and Energy Shielding

Samhain, with its transformative energy and heightened spiritual presence, provides the perfect setting for reinforcing personal protection and building energetic shields. As the veil between worlds thins, it becomes essential to safeguard not just your home but also your own energy and well-being. This chapter focuses on spells designed to protect you from negative influences, psychic attacks, and unwanted energies. By using elements from the natural world and the magic of Samhain, these spells create powerful personal shields and wards.

Each of the 50 spells in this chapter, including "Autumn Aura Shield" and "Samhain Cloak of Shadows," aims to provide you with a protective barrier that can be called upon in daily life, during times of stress, or in situations where you need extra spiritual armor. Whether you need a quick boost to your personal shield or a more complex ritual for long-term protection, these spells will help you maintain a strong and resilient aura.

451. Autumn Aura Shield

The "Autumn Aura Shield" spell uses the energy of the season to create a protective barrier around your personal energy field, deflecting negativity and unwanted influences.

What You Need:

- A handful of autumn leaves (symbolizing transformation and protection)
- A piece of black fabric (to represent a shield)
- A pinch of salt (for purification)
- A small piece of black tourmaline or obsidian (to absorb negative energy)

Steps:

1. **Create Your Space:** Find a quiet place where you can sit comfortably. Place the black fabric in front of you, and arrange the leaves, salt, and stone around it.
2. **Build the Shield:** Hold the autumn leaves in your hands and close your eyes. Visualize a protective shield forming around you, made of golden light and autumn leaves swirling in the

air. Feel this shield growing stronger, creating a barrier that deflects any negativity that comes your way.

3. **Speak the Incantation:** Say aloud, "Leaves of autumn, strong and bold, shield me now, protection unfold. Salt of earth, stone of night, guard my aura, hold it tight."

4. **Place the Leaves:** Lay the leaves onto the black fabric and sprinkle a pinch of salt over them. Place the stone in the center, focusing on its protective energy enhancing your shield.

5. **Close the Ritual:** Fold the fabric around the leaves and stone, forming a small bundle. Keep this bundle in your bag or near you to maintain your shield throughout the season.

452. Samhain Cloak of Shadows

The "Samhain Cloak of Shadows" spell creates an energetic cloak that envelops you in protective shadows, making you less visible to those with ill intentions and shielding you from psychic attacks.

What You Need:

- A black candle (for protection and shadows)
- A sprig of rosemary (for purification and protection)
- A small piece of onyx or obsidian (to absorb negative energy)
- A pinch of dried sage

Steps:

1. **Light the Candle:** In a dimly lit room, light the black candle. Place the rosemary, stone, and dried sage around the candle.

2. **Visualize the Cloak:** Close your eyes and visualize a dark, protective cloak wrapping around you. Imagine it blending with the shadows, making you invisible to negativity and psychic attacks.

3. **Speak the Incantation:** Say, "Cloak of shadows, hide my light, shield me from unwanted sight. In darkness deep, I safely dwell, protected by this Samhain spell."

4. **Anoint with Sage:** Take a pinch of dried sage and rub it gently on the onyx or obsidian stone, then hold the stone in your hands. Feel the energy of the cloak merging with the stone's protective properties.
5. **Close the Spell:** Blow out the candle to seal the spell, and carry the stone with you as a talisman of your protective cloak.

453. Salt and Rosemary Circle
What You Need:

- Sea salt
- Dried rosemary

Steps:

1. **Create the Circle:** Sprinkle a circle of salt and rosemary around yourself, visualizing a protective barrier forming.
2. **Speak the Spell:** Say, "Circle of salt, circle of green, shield my body, keep me unseen."
3. **Close the Circle:** Step out of the circle, leaving the energy in place as a protective barrier.

454. Amulet of Protection
What You Need:

- A piece of black tourmaline
- A small black pouch
- A pinch of salt

Steps:

1. **Cleanse the Stone:** Sprinkle salt over the tourmaline, saying, "Stone of night, absorb all harm, protect me now, keep me warm."

2. **Place in the Pouch:** Put the tourmaline in the black pouch and keep it with you to maintain a shield against negativity.

455. Mirror Shield Spell
What You Need:

- A small hand mirror
- A black candle

Steps:

1. **Light the Candle:** Light the black candle and hold the mirror in your hands.
2. **Visualize:** Visualize the mirror creating a shield around you, reflecting negativity away.
3. **Speak the Spell:** Say, "Mirror of light, reflect all ill, shield me now, keep me still."

456. Sage Smoke Shield
What You Need:

- Dried sage
- A fireproof bowl

Steps:

1. **Light the Sage:** Light the sage and allow it to smolder.
2. **Pass Through Smoke:** Move the bowl around your body, focusing on the smoke creating a protective aura around you.

457. Saltwater Bath Ritual
What You Need:

- Sea salt
- Rosemary oil

Steps:

1. **Prepare the Bath:** Add sea salt and a few drops of rosemary oil to your bath.
2. **Visualize:** As you soak, imagine a shield of light forming around your body.
3. **Speak the Incantation:** Say, "Water of life, salt so pure, protect my spirit, forever endure."

458. Grounding Stone Spell
What You Need:

- A piece of hematite or black tourmaline

Steps:

1. **Hold the Stone:** Sit comfortably, holding the stone in your hand.
2. **Visualize:** Visualize roots growing from the stone into the earth, grounding you and creating a protective barrier.

459. Basil and Mint Pouch
What You Need:

- A small pouch
- Dried basil and mint

Steps:

1. **Fill the Pouch:** Place the basil and mint into the pouch, saying, "Herbs of green, shield my being, protect my spirit, keep me unseen."
2. **Carry the Pouch:** Carry the pouch with you for ongoing protection.

460. Iron Nail Protection
What You Need:

- An iron nail

Steps:

1. **Carry the Nail:** Keep the iron nail in your pocket as a talisman of personal protection.

461-500. Additional Personal Protection Spells
Here are brief overviews of more personal protection spells using the magic of Samhain:
461. Black Ribbon Knot – Tie nine knots in a black ribbon, wear it around your wrist for protection.
462. Salt Circle Shield – Sprinkle a circle of salt around yourself, visualizing it forming a protective barrier.
463. Rosemary Anointing – Rub rosemary oil on your wrists to create an aura of protection.
464. Onyx Cloak Spell – Hold an onyx stone, visualize it forming a cloak around you.
465. Sage Anointing Oil – Anoint your forehead with sage oil for personal shielding.
466. Herb Protection Pouch – Fill a pouch with rosemary, sage, and salt; carry it with you.
467. Moon Water Shield – Anoint your body with moon water for an extra layer of protection.
468. Candle of Shadows – Light a black candle, visualize a shadow cloak forming around you.
469. Iron Ring Ward – Wear an iron ring to ward off psychic attacks.
470. Pine Needle Charm – Create a charm bag with pine needles for protection.
471. Salt and Sage Bath – Bathe in sea salt and sage to cleanse and shield your aura.
472. Pentacle Drawing – Draw a pentacle on a piece of paper, carry it for ongoing protection.
473. Clover Protection – Carry a four-leaf clover in your pocket to ward off negativity.

474. Amethyst Shield – Hold an amethyst stone, visualize its energy forming a shield.

475. Candle Circle Spell – Light four black candles, placing them around you to create a protective circle.

476. Lavender and Salt – Sprinkle lavender and salt in your shoes for ongoing protection.

477. Obsidian Protection – Keep an obsidian stone in your pocket to absorb negative energies.

478. Rosemary Circle – Draw a circle with rosemary around yourself to shield from harm.

479. Basil Anointing – Anoint your chest with basil oil for personal strength and protection.

480. Knot of Warding – Tie a knot in a black ribbon, carry it for daily protection.

481. Protective Sigil – Draw a protective sigil on a small stone, keep it in your bag.

482. Warding Oil – Mix rosemary and sage oils, anoint your wrists and neck for protection.

483. Crystal Grid – Create a grid with black tourmaline and clear quartz on your altar.

484. Sage Smoke Circle – Use sage smoke to form a circle of protection around your body.

485. Herb Necklace – Wear a necklace with a small pouch of rosemary and salt.

486. Pinecone Spell – Carry a small pinecone for personal protection.

487. Apple Blossom Anointing – Rub apple blossom oil on your forehead for spiritual shielding.

488. Candle Flame Shield – Light a candle, visualize its flame forming a shield around you.

489. Amulet of Light – Wear an amulet charged with protective intentions.

490. Warding Knot – Knot a piece of black thread, focusing on its protective power.

491. Grounding Ritual – Stand barefoot on the earth, visualize its energy shielding you.

492. Moonstone Protection – Carry a moonstone to ward off negative energy.

493. Morning Dew Spell – Collect morning dew, anoint your third eye for protection.

494. Cedar Smoke Shield – Burn cedar to create a protective aura.

495. Witch's Ladder – Create a witch's ladder with black and white beads, focusing on protection.

496. Salt and Rosemary Bath – Bathe with salt and rosemary to cleanse and shield your aura.

497. Clover Leaf Shield – Keep a clover leaf in your pocket as a natural shield.

498. Sigil Drawing – Draw a protective sigil on your body with oil.

499. Mirror Reflection – Use a mirror to reflect negative energy away from you.

500. Saltwater Anointing – Anoint your body with saltwater to purify and protect your energy.

These personal protection spells tap into the energy of Samhain to create powerful barriers against negative influences, ensuring your spiritual and physical safety. By using elements of the season and nature's protective symbols, these spells help you maintain a strong and resilient aura, keeping you safe from harm and negativity.

Chapter 16: Banishing Negative Energies (501-550): Spells to Remove Negativity

Samhain, a time when the veil between worlds is at its thinnest, is perfect for banishing unwanted energies, harmful influences, and negative entities. As the dark half of the year approaches, it is crucial to clear away negativity from your life, home, and spirit, creating a space for positive energy to flow. The spells in this chapter are tailored to remove negative forces, cleanse auras, and enhance your personal environment by banishing energies that may be holding you back.

These 50 spells use a variety of elements, such as herbs, candles, salt, water, and the potent energy of Samhain, to cleanse your surroundings and expel unwanted influences. Whether you need to clear your home, protect your aura, or break free from harmful patterns, the following spells—including the "Banishing Mist Spell" and the "Evil Eye Reflector"—offer a range of powerful options to suit your needs.

501. Banishing Mist Spell

The "Banishing Mist Spell" uses a blend of cleansing herbs and essential oils to create a mist that purifies the air, removes negative energies, and creates a sense of peace and clarity in your space.

What You Need:

- A small spray bottle
- Water (preferably moon-charged)
- A few drops of sage essential oil (for purification)
- A few drops of rosemary essential oil (for protection)
- A pinch of sea salt (for banishing negativity)

Steps:

1. **Prepare the Mist:** Fill the spray bottle with water. Add a few drops of sage and rosemary essential oils, and a pinch of sea salt. Shake the bottle gently to mix the ingredients.
2. **Charge the Mist:** Hold the bottle in your hands, close your eyes, and visualize white light pouring into the bottle, infusing the water with cleansing energy. Focus on the intention of banishing negative energies from your space.

3. **Speak the Incantation:** Say, "Mist of sage and rosemary, cleanse this place, banish negativity, leave no trace."
4. **Use the Mist:** Spray the mist around your home, focusing on corners, doorways, and windows where negative energy might linger. As you spray, visualize the mist driving away all negativity, leaving your space feeling refreshed and protected.
5. **Store for Future Use:** Keep the mist in a safe place and use it whenever you feel the need to cleanse and banish negativity from your environment.

502. Evil Eye Reflector

The "Evil Eye Reflector" spell creates a protective barrier around you that not only wards off the evil eye but also reflects any negativity back to its source.

What You Need:

- A small mirror (to reflect negativity)
- A black candle (to absorb negative energy)
- A piece of black ribbon
- A pinch of salt (for purification)

Steps:

1. **Cleanse the Mirror:** Sprinkle a pinch of salt onto the mirror to cleanse it of any previous energies. Wipe it off with a cloth, focusing on your intention to turn the mirror into a reflector of negativity.
2. **Prepare the Candle:** Light the black candle and place it next to the mirror. As the candle burns, visualize it absorbing all the negative energies directed toward you.
3. **Tie the Ribbon:** Wrap the black ribbon around the mirror, tying it securely. As you do so, say, "Mirror bright, reflect the eye, turn all harm back, let peace reside."
4. **Activate the Reflector:** Hold the mirror in your hands and focus on it becoming a shield that deflects all negative intentions away from you. Visualize it sending harmful energies back to their source.

5. **Place the Mirror:** Place the mirror near your front door or in a room where you feel negativity lingers. You can also carry it with you in a bag or pocket for personal protection.

503. Salt and Rosemary Purification
What You Need:

- Sea salt
- Dried rosemary

Steps:

1. **Create the Mixture:** Mix the salt and rosemary in a small bowl. Focus on their purifying and protective properties.
2. **Sprinkle in Corners:** Sprinkle the mixture in the corners of each room, saying, "Salt and rosemary, purify this space, banish all harm, leave only grace."

504. Candle Flame Banishing
What You Need:

- A black candle
- A piece of paper and pen

Steps:

1. **Write the Negativity:** Write down the negative energy or situation you wish to banish on the piece of paper.
2. **Burn the Paper:** Light the black candle and use its flame to burn the paper. As it burns, say, "By this flame, I banish thee, negativity, you have no power over me."

505. Banishing Stone Spell
What You Need:

- A piece of black tourmaline
- A small bowl of saltwater

Steps:

1. **Charge the Stone:** Hold the black tourmaline in your hands and visualize it absorbing negative energies.
2. **Submerge in Saltwater:** Place the stone in the saltwater overnight to cleanse it and charge it with the intention of banishing negativity.

506. Herb Smoke Cleansing
What You Need:

- Dried rosemary, sage, and thyme
- A fireproof bowl

Steps:

1. **Light the Herbs:** Place the herbs in the bowl and light them, allowing them to smolder and produce smoke.
2. **Pass Through Smoke:** Move the bowl around your space, letting the smoke cleanse and banish negativity.

507. Protective Knot Spell
What You Need:

- A piece of black ribbon

Steps:

1. **Tie Nine Knots:** As you tie each knot in the ribbon, focus on different aspects of negativity you wish to banish.
2. **Speak the Spell:** Say, "Nine knots I tie, to banish and bind, negativity, you're out of my mind."

508. Banishing Sigil
What You Need:

- A piece of paper
- A black pen

Steps:

1. **Draw the Sigil:** Draw a sigil representing banishment on the paper.
2. **Burn the Sigil:** Light a black candle and burn the paper with the sigil, visualizing negativity dissolving.

509. Saltwater Bath
What You Need:

- Sea salt
- A few drops of sage oil

Steps:

1. **Prepare the Bath:** Add sea salt and sage oil to your bathwater.
2. **Soak:** As you soak, imagine the water drawing out and banishing all negative energies from your body.

510. Pumpkin Seed Banisher
What You Need:

- A handful of pumpkin seeds
- A small bag

Steps:

1. **Charge the Seeds:** Hold the pumpkin seeds and focus on them absorbing negativity.
2. **Scatter the Seeds:** Scatter the seeds around your property to create a protective barrier.

511-550. Additional Banishing Spells

Here are more spells for banishing negative energies using the magic of Samhain:

511. Pine Needle Scatter – Scatter pine needles around your home to cleanse and banish negativity.

512. Black Candle Circle – Light four black candles, placing them in each corner of a room to banish negative energy.

513. Iron Nail Banishment – Drive an iron nail into the ground near your front door to banish harmful energies.

514. Lavender and Salt Bath – Add lavender and salt to your bath to banish negativity and refresh your aura.

515. Vinegar Floor Wash – Mix vinegar and rosemary in water, mop your floors to cleanse your home.

516. Fire Burn Ritual – Write your negative emotions on paper, burn them in a candle flame.

517. Basil and Mint Pouch – Create a pouch with basil and mint to carry for personal banishment.

518. Wind Banisher – Go outside on a windy day, speak your negative thoughts, let the wind carry them away.

519. Moonlight Purge – Leave a bowl of saltwater under the moon, use it to anoint your body.

520. Herb Sachet Spell – Fill a sachet with sage and rosemary, hang it near your window.

521. Rosemary Smoke Cleanse – Burn dried rosemary, focusing on the smoke purging negativity.

522. Sunflower Seed Banishment – Place sunflower seeds at each corner of your property.

523. Knot of Release – Tie knots in a ribbon, each knot representing something you wish to banish.

524. Salt Jar Ritual – Fill a jar with salt, bury it outside to trap negativity.

525. Lemon Slice Purge – Place lemon slices in each room to absorb negative energies.

526. Morning Dew Anointing – Collect morning dew, anoint your forehead for a fresh start.

527. Black Stone Banishment – Carry a piece of obsidian to absorb negative energy.

528. Salt and Sage Floor Sweep – Sprinkle salt and sage on the floor, sweep it out the door.

529. Crystal Banishing Grid – Arrange black tourmaline in a grid around your space.

530. Warding Sigil – Draw a sigil of banishment on your door.

531. Banish with Water – Pour saltwater across your doorstep to block negativity.

532. Iron Nail at the Gate – Place an iron nail near the entrance to repel negative energies.

533. Candle Wax Drip – Drip wax from a black candle into water to trap negativity.

534. Smoke Circle – Create a circle of protective smoke around yourself.

535. Salt Ring – Create a ring of salt around your bed for peaceful sleep.

536. Banishment Knotting – Knot a black cord while focusing on banishing specific energies.

537. Apple of Release – Bury an apple to symbolize burying negativity.

538. Vinegar Mist – Mix vinegar with water, spray it around your space.

539. Onyx Stone – Place onyx near your bed for personal protection.

540. Sage and Salt Door Sweep – Sweep doorways with sage and salt to cleanse.

541. Bay Leaf Burning – Write your negativity on a bay leaf, burn it in a flame.

542. Stone Circle – Place protective stones in a circle around your home.

543. Burning Rosemary – Burn rosemary to cleanse and banish.

544. Knot of Protection – Tie knots in a black thread, hang it near your window.

545. Clover Shield – Carry a four-leaf clover for personal shielding.

546. Iron Chain Banishment – Place a small iron chain near your entrance.

547. Candle Flame Purge – Light a black candle, focus on its flame absorbing negativity.

548. Lavender Doorstep – Place lavender on your doorstep for peace.

549. Night Whisper Banish – Whisper your fears to the night wind.

550. Candle Wax Seal – Pour candle wax on a piece of paper, bury it outside.

These banishing spells use the transformative power of Samhain to remove negativity from your life and surroundings. By aligning with the season's themes of clearing away the old to make room for the new, these rituals help you create a harmonious and positive environment.

Chapter 17: Nightmare Protection Spells (551-600): Spells to Protect Against Bad Dreams

Samhain, with its dark nights and thin veil between worlds, can often stir up intense energies that manifest as nightmares or restless sleep. As the season invites spirits and heightened spiritual activity, it is common for the subconscious to pick up on these influences, leading to unsettling dreams. The spells in this chapter are designed to protect you from nightmares, banish negative dream entities, and create a calm, peaceful atmosphere conducive to restful sleep.

Utilizing the magical properties of herbs, crystals, symbols, and charms, these spells work to weave a shield around you while you sleep, warding off bad dreams and promoting peaceful rest. This chapter includes 50 spells, starting with the "Samhain Dreamcatcher" and "Sleepy Hollow Nightmare Barrier," followed by a variety of other rituals and charms tailored for nightmare protection.

551. Samhain Dreamcatcher

The "Samhain Dreamcatcher" spell creates a physical and spiritual barrier against nightmares by utilizing the protective power of a traditional dreamcatcher infused with the magic of Samhain.

What You Need:

- A dreamcatcher (handmade or store-bought)
- Black or purple ribbon (for protection and spiritual shielding)
- Sage (for purification)
- A small piece of black tourmaline (for absorbing negative energy)
- A few sprigs of lavender (for calming and peaceful sleep)

Steps:

1. **Cleanse the Dreamcatcher:** Hold the dreamcatcher in your hands and pass it through the smoke of burning sage to cleanse it of any unwanted energies. Focus on your intention to transform it into a shield against nightmares.
2. **Weave in Protection:** Using the black or purple ribbon, weave it into the dreamcatcher's web while visualizing it creating a powerful protective shield. As you weave, chant, "Web of dreams, guardian of night, catch the fears, hold them tight."
3. **Add the Lavender:** Attach the sprigs of lavender to the dreamcatcher, either by tying them to the hoop or placing them in the web. This will bring calm and soothing energy to your sleep.
4. **Charge the Stone:** Hold the piece of black tourmaline and focus on it absorbing all negative energies and dream disturbances. Attach the stone to the bottom of the dreamcatcher as a talisman of protection.
5. **Hang the Dreamcatcher:** Place the dreamcatcher above your bed or in a window to catch and dispel nightmares, allowing only positive dreams to pass through.

552. Sleepy Hollow Nightmare Barrier

The "Sleepy Hollow Nightmare Barrier" creates a protective field around your sleeping space using the energies of Samhain to repel nightmares and negative dream entities.

What You Need:

- A black candle (to absorb and banish negativity)
- A bowl of salt (for purification)
- Dried rosemary (for protection)
- A small sachet or pouch
- A few drops of lavender oil (for calming sleep)

Steps:

1. **Create Your Space:** Place the black candle, bowl of salt, rosemary, and pouch on a small table near your bed. Light the black candle to begin the ritual, focusing on its flame dispelling any negative energy from the room.
2. **Prepare the Sachet:** Fill the small pouch with the salt and dried rosemary, adding a few drops of lavender oil. As you do this, say, "Herbs of protection, salt of earth, guard my sleep, give dreams their worth."
3. **Charge the Sachet:** Hold the pouch in your hands and visualize it creating an invisible barrier around your bed, keeping nightmares and restless energies at bay.
4. **Place the Sachet:** Tuck the sachet under your pillow or hang it on your bedpost to maintain the protective barrier throughout the night.
5. **Seal the Spell:** Let the black candle burn for a few minutes while focusing on your intention for peaceful, nightmare-free sleep, then safely extinguish it.

553. Bay Leaf Dream Protection
What You Need:

- A bay leaf
- A black pen

Steps:

1. **Write on the Leaf:** Write "Protection" on the bay leaf with the pen.
2. **Place Under Pillow:** Place the bay leaf under your pillow while saying, "Bay leaf strong, banish night's wrong. Bring peaceful rest, my dreams be blessed."

554. Salt Circle Sleep Ward
What You Need:

- Sea salt
- A small bowl

Steps:

1. **Prepare the Circle:** Sprinkle salt in a circle around your bed or sleeping area.
2. **Speak the Spell:** As you sprinkle, say, "Salt of earth, ward of light, protect my dreams throughout the night."

555. Lavender Pillow Protection
What You Need:

- Dried lavender
- A small sachet

Steps:

1. **Fill the Sachet:** Place the dried lavender in the sachet, saying, "Lavender calm, protect my sleep, soothe my mind, my dreams to keep."
2. **Place in Pillowcase:** Place the sachet inside your pillowcase to promote peaceful sleep.

556. Candle Flame Dream Cleanse
What You Need:

- A white candle (for purity)
- A small piece of paper
- A pen

Steps:

1. **Write the Intention:** Write down your intention for peaceful dreams on the piece of paper.
2. **Burn the Paper:** Light the candle and burn the paper, visualizing the flame purifying your dreamscape.

557. Crystal Dream Shield
What You Need:

- A piece of amethyst (for peace and protection)
- A small bowl of water

Steps:

1. **Charge the Crystal:** Place the amethyst in the bowl of water and leave it under the moonlight overnight.
2. **Place by Bedside:** Keep the charged crystal on your bedside table to create a shield against nightmares.

558. Protective Dream Knot
What You Need:

- A piece of purple ribbon

Steps:

1. **Tie Nine Knots:** As you tie each knot, focus on banishing nightmares and protecting your dreams.
2. **Place Under Pillow:** Place the knotted ribbon under your pillow, saying, "Knots of nine, dreams divine, guard my sleep, all is fine."

559. Dreamtime Cleansing Spray
What You Need:

- A small spray bottle
- Water
- A few drops of lavender and sage oil

Steps:

1. **Prepare the Spray:** Mix water, lavender, and sage oils in the spray bottle.
2. **Spray Your Bed:** Lightly mist your pillow and bedding before sleep, saying, "Spray of peace, cleanse my space, banish dreams that have no place."

560. Pinecone Nightmare Trap
What You Need:

- A small pinecone
- A piece of black ribbon

Steps:

1. **Wrap the Pinecone:** Wrap the ribbon around the pinecone, focusing on its power to trap nightmares.
2. **Place by Bedside:** Place the pinecone near your bed to trap and neutralize negative dreams.

561-600. Additional Nightmare Protection Spells

Here are more spells for nightmare protection using the magic of Samhain:

561. Salt and Sage Circle – Sprinkle a circle of salt mixed with sage around your bed for protection.

562. Candle Flame Ward – Light a black candle, visualizing it absorbing negative dream energies.

563. Protective Sigil – Draw a sigil for dream protection on paper, place it under your pillow.

564. Moonstone Calm – Keep a moonstone near your bed to bring calming energy.

565. Iron Nail Banishment – Place an iron nail under your bed to ward off bad dreams.

566. Rosemary Pillow Sachet – Create a sachet with rosemary, tuck it in your pillow for protection.

567. Bay Leaf Bed Protection – Place bay leaves under your mattress to ward off nightmares.

568. Morning Dew Anointing – Collect morning dew, anoint your forehead before sleep.

569. Mirror Reflection – Place a small mirror under your bed to reflect nightmares away.

570. Lemon Slice Shield – Place lemon slices near your bed to absorb negative dream energies.

571. Salt Bowl Barrier – Keep a bowl of salt under your bed to trap bad dreams.

572. Candle Wax Seal – Drip black candle wax onto a small stone, place it by your bedside.

573. Amethyst Ward – Keep an amethyst under your pillow for dream protection.

574. Night Whisper Release – Whisper your fears into the night air before sleep to release them.

575. Mint Pillow Spell – Place fresh mint leaves in your pillowcase to deter nightmares.

576. Vinegar Dream Wash – Wash your bedding with water and vinegar to cleanse dream energies.

577. Nightly Knotting – Tie a knot in a ribbon each night, focusing on securing peaceful dreams.

578. Clover Charm – Place a four-leaf clover under your pillow for luck and protection.

579. Herb Pillow Sachet – Create a sachet with lavender, sage, and rosemary for dream protection.

580. Knot of Sleep – Tie nine knots in a white ribbon, place under your pillow for restful sleep.

581. Apple Blossom Anointing – Rub apple blossom oil on your temples before bed.

582. Sunflower Seed Spell – Place sunflower seeds in a bowl by your bed for positivity.

583. Night Candle Protection – Light a white candle for a few minutes before sleep.

584. Crystal Grid – Arrange black tourmaline and clear quartz around your bed for dream shielding.

585. Rosemary Bath – Bathe with rosemary to cleanse your aura before sleep.

586. Knot of Peace – Tie a ribbon with the intention of peace and place it under your pillow.

587. Bay Leaf Knot – Tie a bay leaf into a piece of ribbon, hang it near your bed.

588. Morning Blessing – Upon waking, hold a stone and bless your sleep for the next night.

589. Candle and Sigil – Carve a sigil into a white candle, light it before bed.

590. Sage Smoke Circle – Create a circle of sage smoke around your bed.

591. Nighttime Crystal – Keep a selenite crystal near your bed for tranquility.

592. Lavender Bed Spray – Mix lavender water, spray your bedding.

593. Salt Ring – Sprinkle a ring of salt around your bed.

594. Pine Branch Charm – Hang a small pine branch above your bed.

595. Protective Knot Talisman – Wear a knotted cord around your wrist to bed.

596. Candle Flame Purge – Burn a black candle, visualize nightmares dissipating.

597. Dreamcatcher Knotting – Add knots to a dreamcatcher for extra protection.

598. Night Whisper Sigil – Draw a sigil on paper, speak your intention.

599. Water and Salt Cleanse – Place a bowl of saltwater under your bed.

600. Protective Sleep Oil – Anoint your forehead with rosemary oil.

These nightmare protection spells use the transformative energy of Samhain to create barriers against negative dream forces, ensuring restful and peaceful sleep. By combining elements of the season with traditional protective symbols, these spells empower you to sleep soundly and free of disturbing dreams. May your nights be filled with peace and your dreams remain undisturbed.

Part IV: Healing Spells (601-800)

Chapter 18: Physical Healing Spells (601-650): Spells for Physical Ailments

Samhain marks the end of the harvest season and the beginning of the darker half of the year—a time when our bodies may need extra care and healing. The natural transition into colder weather can often bring physical ailments, making it crucial to harness the healing energies of nature to fortify our physical well-being. The spells in this chapter draw upon the ancient traditions of herbal medicine, energy healing, and magical remedies to address a variety of physical ailments.

By using the natural elements of herbs, essential oils, crystals, and the transformative power of Samhain, these spells can help soothe aches, ease ailments, and promote overall physical healing. This chapter includes 50 spells, starting with the "Healing Harvest Herb Mix" and "Witch's Remedy Brew," followed by additional rituals and concoctions for physical health. These spells should be used as a complementary practice and not a substitute for professional medical treatment.

601. Healing Harvest Herb Mix

The "Healing Harvest Herb Mix" is a powerful blend of seasonal herbs known for their healing properties. This spell combines the magic of Samhain with the natural potency of herbs to promote physical recovery and well-being.

What You Need:

- A small bowl
- Dried rosemary (for purification and healing)
- Dried sage (to cleanse and protect)
- Dried thyme (for strength)
- Dried peppermint (to soothe pain and inflammation)
- A small pouch

Steps:

1. **Prepare Your Space:** Begin by cleansing your space with a sage smudge or incense to clear away negative energies and create a focused, healing environment.

2. **Mix the Herbs:** In the small bowl, combine the dried rosemary, sage, thyme, and peppermint. As you mix, visualize your physical ailment being alleviated and your body being filled with renewed strength and health.

3. **Speak the Healing Spell:** While mixing, chant, "Herbs of earth, strong and pure, lend me strength, bring the cure. Heal my body, ease my pain, bring me health and strength again."

4. **Charge the Mix:** Hold the bowl in your hands and focus on the intention of physical healing, imbuing the herbs with your energy and the healing power of Samhain.

5. **Store in a Pouch:** Transfer the mixed herbs into a small pouch. Keep this pouch under your pillow, near your bedside, or carry it with you to absorb the healing energies.

6. **Use as Needed:** You can open the pouch and inhale the scent of the herbs whenever you feel the need for physical relief or healing. The pouch will continue to emit its healing energy as long as you carry it.

602. Witch's Remedy Brew

The "Witch's Remedy Brew" is a healing potion made from herbal ingredients that work to alleviate physical symptoms and promote bodily health. This brew can be consumed when you're feeling unwell, using the magic of Samhain to boost its efficacy.

What You Need:

- A small pot
- 2 cups of water
- 1 teaspoon dried peppermint (for soothing stomach and muscle pain)
- 1 teaspoon dried rosemary (for boosting immunity)
- 1 teaspoon dried thyme (for respiratory health)
- 1 teaspoon honey (for soothing and healing)
- A pinch of sea salt (for purification)

Steps:

1. **Prepare the Brew:** Pour the water into the pot and bring it to a gentle boil. Add the peppermint, rosemary, and thyme to the pot, stirring clockwise while focusing on your intention for healing.
2. **Infuse with Healing Energy:** Reduce the heat and let the herbs steep for 10 minutes. As they steep, chant, "Herbs of might, brew of cure, bring me health, strong and pure."
3. **Strain and Add Honey:** Strain the mixture into a cup, removing the herbs. Add a teaspoon of honey and a pinch of sea salt, stirring clockwise to infuse the brew with additional healing energy.
4. **Drink the Brew:** Slowly sip the brew while visualizing it spreading warmth and healing throughout your body, easing pain, and strengthening your immune system.
5. **Repeat as Needed:** This remedy brew can be consumed once a day during times of physical discomfort or illness. Store any remaining liquid in a covered container in the refrigerator for up to 2 days.

603. Rosemary Healing Bath
What You Need:

- A handful of fresh or dried rosemary
- Sea salt
- A bathtub filled with warm water

Steps:

1. **Prepare the Bath:** Add the rosemary and a handful of sea salt to the warm bathwater.
2. **Enter the Bath:** Soak in the bath, visualizing the water absorbing any physical pain or discomfort.
3. **Speak the Spell:** Chant, "Rosemary, salt, cleanse my skin, heal my body, strength within."

604. Amethyst Pain Relief
What You Need:

- A small amethyst crystal

Steps:

1. **Hold the Crystal:** Sit comfortably, holding the amethyst in your hands. Close your eyes and visualize the crystal glowing with a healing purple light.
2. **Place on Affected Area:** Gently place the crystal on the area of your body where you feel discomfort, saying, "Amethyst, stone of healing light, ease my pain, make me right."

605. Healing Knot Spell
What You Need:

- A piece of green ribbon (green for healing)

Steps:

1. **Tie Nine Knots:** As you tie each knot, focus on a specific area of your body that needs healing.
2. **Speak the Spell:** Say, "Knot of nine, health be mine, bind the pain, restore and shine."

606. Peppermint Headache Balm
What You Need:

- A few drops of peppermint essential oil
- A small cloth

Steps:

1. **Anoint the Cloth:** Apply a few drops of peppermint oil onto the cloth.
2. **Place on Forehead:** Place the cloth on your forehead, saying, "Peppermint, cool and clear, ease this pain, make it disappear."

607. Healing Candle Ritual
What You Need:

- A green candle
- Rosemary oil

Steps:

1. **Anoint the Candle:** Rub rosemary oil on the candle, focusing on its healing properties.
2. **Light the Candle:** Light the candle, saying, "Flame of green, heal and restore, bring me health, forevermore."

608. Herbal Foot Soak
What You Need:

- A basin of warm water
- Dried chamomile and peppermint
- A handful of sea salt

Steps:

1. **Prepare the Soak:** Add the herbs and salt to the warm water.
2. **Soak Your Feet:** Place your feet in the basin and relax, saying, "Herbs of calm, water so pure, heal my body, pain no more."

609. Healing Stone Circle
What You Need:

- Small healing stones (amethyst, rose quartz, clear quartz)

Steps:

1. **Create a Circle:** Arrange the stones in a circle around you, focusing on their healing energies surrounding and penetrating your body.
2. **Speak the Spell:** Chant, "Stones of healing, stones of light, restore my body, make it right."

610. Herbal Compress
What You Need:

- A handful of fresh mint leaves
- A small cloth

Steps:

1. **Create the Compress:** Place the mint leaves in the cloth, tie it securely.
2. **Apply to Affected Area:** Place the compress on the affected area, saying, "Mint of green, heal my pain, bring relief, health regain."

611-650. Additional Physical Healing Spells

Here are more spells for physical healing using the magic of Samhain:

611. Saltwater Healing Bath – Add sea salt to a warm bath and soak, visualizing the salt drawing out illness.

612. Moon Water Anointing – Anoint your forehead with moon-charged water to promote healing.

613. Sage Smoke Healing – Pass a smoldering sage bundle around your body, focusing on its purifying smoke clearing ailments.

614. Bay Leaf Healing Charm – Write your health wish on a bay leaf, burn it in a flame, visualizing the ailment burning away.

615. Herb Sachet – Create a sachet with rosemary, thyme, and peppermint; carry it with you for ongoing health.

616. Lavender Rest Spell – Place dried lavender under your pillow for restful, healing sleep.

617. Protective Knot – Tie a knot in a white ribbon, wear it around your wrist for ongoing healing.

618. Amethyst Healing – Place an amethyst under your pillow to promote recovery during sleep.

619. Sunlight Infusion – Stand in sunlight, visualizing its rays filling your body with healing warmth.

620. Mint Tea Remedy – Brew mint tea, drink it while visualizing it soothing your body.

621. Crystal Grid – Create a crystal grid with healing stones on your bedside table.

622. Knot of Strength – Tie knots in a green ribbon, each representing an aspect of your health being restored.

623. Salt Circle – Stand in a circle of salt, imagining it cleansing and restoring your body.

624. Healing Candle Circle – Light four green candles, placing them in a circle around you.

625. Bay Leaf Infusion – Boil bay leaves in water, inhale the steam for respiratory relief.

626. Chamomile Compress – Place a chamomile compress on your forehead for headaches.

627. Rose Quartz Bath – Place rose quartz in your bathwater for a soothing effect.

628. Morning Dew Anointing – Collect morning dew, anoint your affected area for healing.

629. Herbal Floor Wash – Mop your home with a rosemary and salt infusion for a healing environment.

630. Moonlight Healing – Sit in moonlight, visualizing it cleansing and healing your body.

631. Herb Knotting – Knot herbs into a fabric, hang it in your room for continuous healing.

632. Candle Flame Healing – Focus on a green candle flame, imagining it burning away illness.

633. Mint Inhalation – Inhale the scent of fresh mint for sinus relief.

634. Healing Circle Ritual – Sit in a circle of stones, focusing on their healing properties.

635. Knot of Light – Tie a white ribbon around your wrist for ongoing health.

636. Apple of Health – Keep an apple by your bedside for continuous health energy.

637. Sage and Salt Wash – Wash your hands with sage-infused saltwater.

638. Lavender Anointing – Rub lavender oil on your temples for calm and healing.

639. Protective Knot Talisman – Wear a knotted cord for health protection.

640. Mint Leaf Healing – Place mint leaves on the affected area.

641. Salt Jar – Keep a jar of salt in your room to absorb illness.

642. Amethyst Cleansing – Hold an amethyst while visualizing it cleansing your ailment.

643. Sunflower Oil – Anoint your skin with sunflower oil for health.

644. Protective Sigil – Draw a healing sigil on paper, keep it under your pillow.

645. Healing Water – Drink moon-charged water for internal healing.

646. Candle Wax Healing – Drip candle wax into water, visualizing your pain melting away.

647. Salt and Rosemary Bath – Soak in a bath with salt and rosemary for full-body healing.

648. Knot of Recovery – Tie knots in a green ribbon, focus on recovery.

649. Sage Bath – Add sage to your bath for a soothing soak.

650. Herb Stone Circle – Place stones and herbs in a circle around you.

These physical healing spells tap into the natural energies of Samhain and the power of herbs, crystals, and intentions to promote recovery and well-being. By aligning with the earth's cycles and harnessing the magic of the season, these spells work to restore health and alleviate physical discomfort. Always remember to use these spells as a complement to professional medical care.

Chapter 19: Emotional Healing Spells (651-700): Spells for Emotional Well-Being

Samhain, a time of deep reflection and transformation, offers an ideal opportunity to focus on emotional healing. As the veil between worlds thins, it's easier to tap into the energies of the spirit realm and the natural world to help mend emotional wounds, release grief, and find inner calm. The following spells draw upon the nurturing power of herbs, crystals, water, and the energies of the season to soothe emotional turmoil, restore balance, and promote peace of mind.

These spells aim to help you work through emotional challenges, whether it's heartache, anxiety, grief, or simply the need for inner calm. From soothing elixirs to comforting baths, each spell in this chapter offers a unique way to address various aspects of emotional well-being. The chapter begins with the "Autumn Calm Elixir" and "Samhain Heart-Healing Bath," then continues with a selection of rituals and charms designed to guide you toward emotional equilibrium.

651. Autumn Calm Elixir

The "Autumn Calm Elixir" is a gentle, soothing potion crafted with herbs known for their calming properties. It is designed to help you relax, release tension, and foster a sense of emotional peace during times of stress and emotional upheaval.

What You Need:

- 1 cup of water
- 1 teaspoon dried chamomile (for relaxation)
- 1 teaspoon dried lavender (for calming the mind)
- 1 teaspoon dried lemon balm (for emotional balance)
- 1 teaspoon honey (to sweeten and soothe)
- A small saucepan
- A strainer
- A cup

Steps:

1. **Prepare Your Space:** Before brewing the elixir, create a peaceful environment by dimming the lights and lighting a candle. This will help set the intention for emotional healing.

2. **Boil the Water:** Pour the water into the small saucepan and bring it to a gentle boil. Add the chamomile, lavender, and lemon balm to the water.

3. **Infuse with Healing:** Reduce the heat and allow the herbs to simmer for 5-10 minutes. As they steep, focus on your intention for emotional calm. Visualize the herbs releasing their soothing energies into the water, filling the elixir with healing properties.

4. **Strain and Add Honey:** After simmering, remove the saucepan from the heat and strain the liquid into a cup. Add a teaspoon of honey, stirring clockwise to blend the sweetness into the elixir.

5. **Drink with Intention:** Sip the elixir slowly, closing your eyes and visualizing its warmth spreading throughout your body, easing emotional tension, and calming your mind. Say the incantation: "Herbs of calm, bring me peace. Heal my heart, let troubles cease."

6. **Repeat as Needed:** This elixir can be made whenever you need emotional support and calm. Store the dried herbs in a sealed container for future use.

652. Samhain Heart-Healing Bath

The "Samhain Heart-Healing Bath" is a nurturing ritual that uses the cleansing properties of water and the healing energies of herbs and oils to soothe emotional wounds. This bath helps release grief, heartache, and emotional stress, replacing it with peace and self-love.

What You Need:

- A handful of dried rose petals (for self-love and emotional healing)
- A handful of dried lavender (to calm and soothe)
- A few drops of rose oil (to open the heart)
- A handful of sea salt (for purification and release)
- A bathtub filled with warm water

Steps:

1. **Prepare the Bath:** Run a warm bath, adding the dried rose petals, lavender, and sea salt to the water. As the tub fills, focus on the intention of emotional healing and release.

2. **Add the Rose Oil:** Add a few drops of rose oil to the bath, stirring the water gently with your hand to disperse it. Visualize the water turning into a healing elixir that will cleanse and soothe your emotional body.

3. **Enter the Bath:** Step into the tub and immerse yourself in the warm, fragrant water. Close your eyes and take deep, calming breaths, allowing the scent of the herbs and oils to fill your senses.

4. **Visualize Healing:** Visualize the water absorbing all your emotional pain, heartache, and grief. Imagine it washing away any heaviness or negativity, leaving you feeling lighter and more at peace.

5. **Speak the Spell:** As you soak, chant softly, "Water of life, petals so fair, heal my heart, dissolve my care. Rose and lavender, bring peace to me, cleanse my spirit, set me free."

6. **Relax and Reflect:** Stay in the bath for at least 15-20 minutes, allowing the herbs and oils to work their magic. Reflect on any emotions that arise, acknowledging them and letting them go.

7. **Conclude the Ritual:** When you're ready, drain the tub, visualizing all your emotional burdens being carried away with the water. Pat yourself dry with a towel, feeling renewed and comforted.

653. Lavender Calm Charm
What You Need:

- A small pouch
- Dried lavender (to soothe anxiety)
- A small piece of rose quartz (for self-love and emotional balance)

Steps:

1. **Fill the Pouch:** Place the dried lavender and rose quartz in the pouch, visualizing the calming and loving energies surrounding you.

2. **Speak the Spell:** Say, "Lavender calm, rose quartz bright, ease my heart, make things right."

3. **Carry the Charm:** Carry the pouch with you for emotional support throughout the day.

654. Emotional Release Candle
What You Need:

- A pink candle (for love and emotional healing)
- Rose oil

Steps:

1. **Anoint the Candle:** Rub rose oil onto the candle, focusing on your intention for emotional release.
2. **Light the Candle:** Light the candle and say, "Candle of pink, burn so bright, ease my heart, bring love and light."
3. **Visualize:** As the candle burns, visualize it melting away your emotional pain and filling you with warmth and peace.

655. Moonlight Healing Ritual
What You Need:

- A small bowl of water
- Rose petals
- A few drops of lavender oil

Steps:

1. **Prepare the Bowl:** Place the water, rose petals, and lavender oil into the bowl.
2. **Charge Under the Moon:** Place the bowl outside under the light of the full moon to absorb its healing energy.

3. **Anoint Yourself:** Use the moon-charged water to anoint your forehead and heart, saying, "Moonlight pure, heal my heart, bring me peace, let pain depart."

656. Sage Smoke Cleansing
What You Need:

- Dried sage
- A fireproof bowl

Steps:

1. **Light the Sage:** Light the sage and allow it to smolder in the bowl, producing cleansing smoke.
2. **Pass Through Smoke:** Close your eyes and pass the smoke around your body, focusing on it purging any negative emotions.

657. Bay Leaf Release
What You Need:

- A bay leaf
- A pen
- A fireproof bowl

Steps:

1. **Write on the Leaf:** Write the emotional pain or grief you wish to release on the bay leaf.
2. **Burn the Leaf:** Light the bay leaf and place it in the fireproof bowl, saying, "By this flame, I release my pain, cleanse my heart, peace remain."

658. Crystal Heart Grid
What You Need:

- Rose quartz, amethyst, and clear quartz crystals

Steps:

1. **Arrange the Grid:** Place the crystals in a heart-shaped grid on your altar or bedside table.
2. **Speak the Spell:** Say, "Crystals of love, crystals of light, heal my heart, bring peace this night."

659. Knot of Emotional Strength
What You Need:

- A piece of pink ribbon

Steps:

1. **Tie Nine Knots:** As you tie each knot, focus on different aspects of your emotional strength.
2. **Carry the Ribbon:** Carry the ribbon with you, saying, "Knots of nine, peace be mine, strength within, love divine."

660. Peppermint Tea for Grief
What You Need:

- 1 teaspoon dried peppermint
- 1 cup of boiling water
- A teaspoon of honey

Steps:

1. **Brew the Tea:** Add the peppermint to the boiling water and steep for 5 minutes.
2. **Add Honey:** Stir in honey, saying, "Peppermint bright, bring me peace, ease my grief, let pain release."

661-700. Additional Emotional Healing Spells

Here are additional spells for emotional healing using the magic of Samhain:

661. Rosemary Heart Balm – Mix rosemary oil with a carrier oil, rub on your chest for emotional balance.

662. Salt Circle – Stand in a circle of salt, imagining it cleansing your emotions.

663. Sunlight Meditation – Sit in sunlight, focusing on its warmth healing your emotional wounds.

664. Rose Petal Sachet – Create a sachet with rose petals, carry it for self-love.

665. Candle of Peace – Light a white candle, visualizing peace filling your heart.

666. Apple Blossom Anointing – Anoint your wrists with apple blossom oil for comfort.

667. Lavender Pillow – Place dried lavender under your pillow for restful sleep.

668. Knot of Calm – Tie a knot in a white ribbon, carry it for emotional strength.

669. Amethyst Water – Soak an amethyst in water, use it to wash your hands.

670. Morning Dew Blessing – Anoint your heart with morning dew for calm.

671. Rose Quartz Meditation – Meditate while holding rose quartz, visualizing its energy healing your heart.

672. Bay Leaf Heart – Write "Love" on a bay leaf, place it under your pillow.

673. Peppermint Inhalation – Inhale peppermint oil for emotional refreshment.

674. Crystal Grid – Create a crystal grid with rose quartz around your bed.

675. Herbal Floor Wash – Mop your home with rosemary and lavender infusion.

676. Candlelight Reflection – Sit by candlelight, focusing on the flame soothing your emotions.

677. Saltwater Bath – Add salt to your bath to cleanse emotional pain.

678. Lavender Knot – Tie lavender into a ribbon, keep it in your pocket.

679. Pinecone Comfort – Keep a pinecone by your bed for emotional stability.

680. Moon Water Anointing – Anoint your third eye with moon-charged water.

681. Herb Knotting – Knot herbs into a cloth, hang it in your room.

682. Candle Wax Release – Drip candle wax onto paper, visualizing it absorbing your pain.

683. Morning Ritual – Hold a crystal at sunrise, setting an intention for peace.

684. Rose Bath – Add rose petals to your bath.

685. Rosemary Smudge – Smudge your room with rosemary smoke.

686. Apple of Healing – Keep an apple by your bedside.

687. Knot of Strength – Tie a pink ribbon around your wrist.

688. Sage Infusion – Brew sage tea, sip slowly for inner calm.

689. Lavender Water Spray – Mix lavender oil with water, spray your room.

690. Heart Crystal Circle – Place crystals in a circle around your heart.

691. Peppermint Rest – Place peppermint leaves under your pillow.

692. Candlelit Calm – Meditate by candlelight.

693. Lavender Oil – Anoint your temples.

694. Rose Quartz Bath – Place rose quartz in bathwater.

695. Sunflower Oil – Anoint your skin with sunflower oil.

696. Moonlit Meditation – Meditate under moonlight.

697. Crystal Knotting – Knot a crystal into a ribbon.

698. Apple Blossom Spell – Anoint your heart with oil.

699. Salt and Rose Bath – Bathe with salt and rose petals.

700. Knot of Release – Tie knots in a ribbon.

These emotional healing spells harness the nurturing power of Samhain and the natural elements to promote emotional balance and inner peace. By embracing the season's transformative energy, these rituals help you work through emotional challenges and open your heart to self-love and tranquility. Use these spells to find comfort, heal wounds, and cultivate a peaceful state of mind.

Chapter 20: Spiritual Healing Spells (701-750): Spells for Spiritual Restoration

Samhain is a time of profound spiritual renewal when the veil between the physical world and the spirit realm is at its thinnest. This liminal period offers an opportunity for deep spiritual reflection, growth, and restoration. The spells in this chapter focus on spiritual healing, helping you release spiritual burdens, restore inner harmony, and reconnect with your higher self. They draw upon the essence of the season—harvest, transformation, and the descent into the introspective winter months.

Spiritual healing involves cleansing the spirit of past traumas, restoring energy balance, and strengthening the connection with your inner truth and the divine. Through the use of herbs, crystals, meditation, and ritual, these spells are crafted to facilitate your spiritual journey. This chapter begins with "Soul Renewal Ritual" and "Pumpkin Essence Meditation," followed by additional spells for spiritual restoration that you can perform during Samhain or any time you seek spiritual healing.

701. Soul Renewal Ritual

The "Soul Renewal Ritual" is a powerful ceremony that utilizes the transformative energy of Samhain to cleanse, heal, and rejuvenate your spirit. This ritual helps release spiritual blockages, past traumas, and negative energy that may be holding you back, allowing for a renewed sense of spiritual clarity and purpose.

What You Need:

- A black candle (for banishing negativity)
- A white candle (for purity and spiritual renewal)
- A small bowl of water (for cleansing)
- A pinch of sea salt (for purification)
- Dried sage (for cleansing)
- A sprig of rosemary (for spiritual protection)
- A small amethyst crystal (for spiritual clarity)

Steps:

1. **Create Your Sacred Space:** Find a quiet place where you won't be disturbed. Cleanse the area with burning sage, focusing on clearing away any lingering negative energies.
2. **Set Up Your Altar:** Place the black candle on the left and the white candle on the right. Set the bowl of water with the pinch of sea salt in front of you. Place the rosemary and amethyst nearby.
3. **Light the Candles:** Light the black candle first, saying, "Flame of shadow, banish despair. Burn away burdens, free my spirit's air." Next, light the white candle, saying, "Flame of light, renew my soul. Fill me with peace, make me whole."
4. **Cleanse with Water:** Dip your fingers into the saltwater and sprinkle it over your heart, saying, "Water of life, wash away strife. Cleanse my spirit, renew my light."
5. **Hold the Amethyst:** Pick up the amethyst crystal and hold it in your hands. Close your eyes and visualize a radiant purple light surrounding you, filling you with spiritual clarity and peace.
6. **Charge the Rosemary:** Take the sprig of rosemary and hold it over the flames of both candles, allowing it to absorb their energies. Say, "Herb of wisdom, herb of grace, guard my spirit, hold my space."
7. **Close the Ritual:** Extinguish the black candle first, symbolizing the release of negativity. Leave the white candle burning for a few more minutes to fill the space with pure, renewing energy. Once you feel ready, extinguish the white candle, sealing the ritual.
8. **Keep the Crystal:** Carry the amethyst with you or place it on your altar to maintain the spiritual clarity gained from this ritual.

702. Pumpkin Essence Meditation

The "Pumpkin Essence Meditation" draws upon the seasonal energy of pumpkins, which symbolize abundance, protection, and spiritual growth. This meditation helps you ground yourself, reconnect with your inner essence, and draw strength from the natural world.

What You Need:

- A small pumpkin
- A comfortable place to sit
- A quiet environment
- A blanket (optional, for comfort)

Steps:

1. **Create a Calming Space:** Find a quiet and comfortable spot where you can sit undisturbed. Place the pumpkin in front of you, either on the ground or on a small table.
2. **Begin the Meditation:** Sit comfortably with your hands resting on your knees, palms facing up. Close your eyes and take several deep breaths, allowing yourself to relax and center your mind.
3. **Visualize the Pumpkin's Energy:** With each breath, imagine the energy of the pumpkin filling the space around you. Visualize a warm, golden-orange light emanating from the pumpkin, surrounding you with a sense of comfort and safety.
4. **Absorb the Essence:** As you breathe in, imagine drawing this golden light into your body. Feel it traveling through your veins, reaching every part of your being, and restoring your spiritual energy.
5. **Grounding with the Earth:** Visualize roots growing from your body into the earth, connecting you to the ground beneath you. Feel the strength and support of the earth flowing into your body, grounding and centering your spirit.
6. **Focus on Healing:** Spend several minutes in this state of meditation, focusing on the warm, healing energy filling your spirit. Allow any spiritual pain, confusion, or negativity to dissolve into the light.

7. **Close the Meditation:** When you're ready, slowly bring your awareness back to the present moment. Open your eyes and take a deep breath. You can place the pumpkin on your altar or in a prominent place in your home to serve as a reminder of the spiritual connection you established during this meditation.

703. Sage and Rosemary Smudge
What You Need:

- Dried sage (for purification)
- Dried rosemary (for spiritual protection)
- A fireproof bowl

Steps:

1. **Light the Smudge:** Place the sage and rosemary in the fireproof bowl and light them, allowing them to smolder and produce smoke.
2. **Cleanse Your Aura:** Pass the smoke around your body, focusing on its purifying properties. Say, "Smoke of sage, herb of grace, cleanse my spirit, clear my space."

704. Salt Circle Spiritual Cleansing
What You Need:

- Sea salt
- A small bowl of water

Steps:

1. **Create the Circle:** Sprinkle a circle of sea salt around you. Place the bowl of water in the center.

2. **Cleanse with Saltwater:** Dip your fingers into the water and anoint your forehead, saying, "Salt of earth, water pure, cleanse my spirit, make it sure."

705. Crystal Grid for Spiritual Clarity
What You Need:

- Clear quartz (for clarity)
- Amethyst (for spiritual insight)
- Rose quartz (for emotional balance)

Steps:

1. **Arrange the Grid:** Place the crystals in a triangular shape, with clear quartz at the top, amethyst on the left, and rose quartz on the right.
2. **Activate the Grid:** Focus on the crystals, visualizing a beam of light connecting them. Say, "Crystals bright, guide my sight, heal my spirit, bring me light."

706. Candle Flame Meditation
What You Need:

- A white candle (for purity)
- A quiet space

Steps:

1. **Light the Candle:** Place the candle in front of you and light it.
2. **Focus on the Flame:** Sit comfortably and gaze at the flame, allowing its light to fill your mind. Visualize it burning away any spiritual impurities.

707. Bay Leaf Spiritual Release
What You Need:

- A bay leaf
- A pen
- A fireproof bowl

Steps:

1. **Write on the Leaf:** Write down any spiritual burdens you wish to release on the bay leaf.
2. **Burn the Leaf:** Light the bay leaf and place it in the fireproof bowl, saying, "Bay leaf burn, burdens gone, clear my spirit, light of dawn."

708. Rose Petal Spiritual Bath
What You Need:

- A handful of dried rose petals
- A few drops of lavender oil
- A bathtub filled with warm water

Steps:

1. **Prepare the Bath:** Add the rose petals and lavender oil to the bathwater.
2. **Soak:** Enter the bath, focusing on the water purifying and soothing your spirit. Say, "Water pure, roses bright, cleanse my soul, bring me light."

709. Protective Knot Spell
What You Need:

- A piece of purple ribbon

Steps:

1. **Tie Nine Knots:** As you tie each knot, focus on your intention for spiritual protection and renewal.
2. **Wear the Ribbon:** Keep the ribbon with you, saying, "Knot of nine, guard my soul, bring me peace, make me whole."

710. Amethyst Healing Meditation
What You Need:

- An amethyst crystal

Steps:

1. **Hold the Crystal:** Sit comfortably, holding the amethyst in your hand.
2. **Visualize:** Close your eyes and visualize the crystal's energy enveloping your spirit, clearing away negativity.

711-750. Additional Spiritual Healing Spells
Here are additional spells for spiritual healing using the energy of Samhain:

711. Moon Water Anointing – Anoint your forehead with moon-charged water for spiritual clarity.

712. Saltwater Circle – Stand in a circle of salt, visualizing it purifying your spirit.

713. Lavender Oil Anointing – Rub lavender oil on your temples to calm your spirit.

714. Rose Quartz Meditation – Meditate while holding rose quartz, focusing on self-love.

715. Candle of Peace – Light a white candle, visualizing its flame purifying your aura.

716. Herb Pouch – Create a pouch with rosemary and sage for spiritual protection.

717. Salt Bath – Add sea salt to your bath for spiritual cleansing.

718. Knot of Light – Tie a white ribbon, focusing on spiritual restoration.

719. Morning Sun Ritual – Stand in sunlight, visualizing it filling your spirit with warmth.

720. Sage Smoke – Smudge your room with sage to clear spiritual clutter.

721. Rose Water Anointing – Anoint your heart with rose water for self-love.

722. Crystal Grid – Arrange clear quartz and amethyst in a grid on your altar.

723. Morning Dew Anointing – Anoint your third eye with morning dew for clarity.

724. Candle Flame Meditation – Gaze into a candle flame to focus your spirit.

725. Lavender Sachet – Create a sachet with lavender, carry it for spiritual calm.

726. Herb Knotting – Knot rosemary and sage into a cloth, hang it near your bed.

727. Saltwater Anointing – Anoint your forehead with saltwater.

728. Rose Petal Blessing – Scatter rose petals around your altar.

729. Apple Blossom Anointing – Use apple blossom oil on your wrists.

730. Sun Meditation – Meditate in sunlight.

731. Crystal Cleansing – Hold a clear quartz to cleanse your aura.

732. Knot of Strength – Tie a ribbon, focusing on spiritual strength.

733. Candle of Light – Burn a white candle for spiritual purification.

734. Herb Sachet – Carry a sachet with herbs for spiritual healing.

735. Moon Bath – Bathe in moonlight for spiritual cleansing.

736. Lavender Circle – Create a circle with lavender around you.

737. Crystal Knot – Knot a crystal into a ribbon for protection.

738. Candle Flame – Focus on the candle flame.

739. Saltwater Bath – Add salt to your bath.

740. Herb Circle – Create a circle with herbs.

741. Morning Dew – Anoint yourself.

742. Knot Spell – Tie knots.

743. Moonlight Meditation – Meditate under the moon.

744. Apple Blossom Spell – Anoint yourself.

745. Rose Quartz Bath – Place rose quartz in your bath.

746. Candle Anointing – Anoint a candle with oil.

747. Knot of Calm – Tie a ribbon for calm.

748. Lavender Anointing – Use lavender.

749. Crystal Light – Meditate.

750. Salt Circle – Stand in a circle.

These spiritual healing spells harness the power of Samhain to cleanse, restore, and uplift your spirit. By aligning with the natural elements and the season's transformative energy, these rituals facilitate a deep spiritual renewal. Use these spells to release burdens, gain clarity, and strengthen your connection to your inner self and the divine.

Chapter 21: Energy Cleansing Spells (751-800): Spells to Cleanse Your Aura and Energy

Samhain, with its potent transformational energies, is an ideal time to cleanse and refresh your personal energy field, known as the aura. As we transition into the darker half of the year, it's important to clear away stagnant energies, negativity, and spiritual debris that may have accumulated in our auras. By removing these blockages, we make space for positive energy, enhance our spiritual strength, and promote overall well-being.

Energy cleansing spells use the purifying powers of herbs, crystals, water, and light to renew and protect your aura. This chapter focuses on techniques to cleanse your personal energy field and reset your vibrational state. Beginning with the "Samhain Smoke Purification" and "Crystal Energy Clearing," this chapter offers a variety of detailed rituals and spells to restore and maintain energetic harmony.

751. Samhain Smoke Purification

The "Samhain Smoke Purification" is a traditional cleansing ritual that utilizes the smoke of sacred herbs to purify your aura, release negativity, and restore balance. This spell draws on the powerful cleansing properties of herbs commonly associated with Samhain, such as sage and rosemary.

What You Need:

- A bundle of dried sage (for purification)
- A few sprigs of dried rosemary (for spiritual protection)
- A fireproof bowl or abalone shell
- A lighter or matches

Steps:

1. **Create Your Sacred Space:** Find a quiet, comfortable space where you can perform this cleansing. Open a window or door to allow negative energy to leave.

2. **Light the Herbs:** Hold the sage and rosemary bundle over the fireproof bowl and light it with the lighter or matches. Allow the herbs to smolder and produce smoke. If the flame grows too strong, gently blow it out to keep a steady stream of smoke.

3. **Begin the Cleansing:** Stand in the center of your space, holding the smoking herbs in one hand and the fireproof bowl in the other. Slowly move the bundle around your body, starting at your feet and working your way up to your head. As you do this, visualize the smoke absorbing any negative or stagnant energy from your aura.

4. **Speak the Incantation:** As you move the smoke around your body, say, "Smoke of sage, purify my light. Rosemary strong, guard my night. Cleanse my aura, make it bright. Energy clear, pure and right."

5. **Clear Your Space:** After purifying your aura, move around the room, using the smoke to cleanse the corners, doorways, and windows. Visualize the smoke driving out any negative energies from your surroundings.

6. **Close the Ritual:** When you feel the space and your aura have been cleansed, extinguish the bundle safely in the fireproof bowl. Take a deep breath and feel the renewed sense of clarity and lightness in your energy field.

752. Crystal Energy Clearing

"Crystal Energy Clearing" uses the power of crystals to cleanse and rejuvenate your aura. Crystals like selenite and clear quartz are particularly effective in absorbing negative energy and restoring vibrational harmony.

What You Need:

- A selenite wand (for clearing and raising vibrations)
- A piece of clear quartz (for amplification)
- A comfortable place to sit

Steps:

1. **Prepare the Space:** Find a quiet place where you can sit comfortably without interruptions. Hold the selenite wand in your dominant hand and the clear quartz in your other hand.
2. **Begin the Cleansing:** Close your eyes and take a few deep breaths to center yourself. Slowly move the selenite wand from the top of your head down to your feet, as if you are combing through your aura. Visualize the wand absorbing and breaking up any stagnant or negative energy within your energy field.
3. **Repeat the Process:** Move the selenite wand around your body, paying extra attention to areas where you feel tension or heaviness. Afterward, hold the clear quartz against your heart, focusing on it amplifying positive energy within your aura.
4. **Speak the Incantation:** As you continue this process, chant, "Crystal light, pure and clear, cleanse my energy, release all fear. Selenite bright, quartz so pure, cleanse my aura, make it sure."
5. **Close the Ritual:** When you feel your aura is cleansed and renewed, place the crystals on your altar or in a sacred space. Take a moment to reflect on the sense of peace and clarity within your energy field.

753. Saltwater Cleansing Bath
What You Need:

- A bathtub filled with warm water
- A handful of sea salt (for purification)
- A few drops of lavender oil (for soothing and calming)

Steps:

1. **Prepare the Bath:** Add the sea salt and lavender oil to the warm bathwater, stirring gently with your hand to disperse the ingredients.

2. **Soak and Cleanse:** Enter the bath, closing your eyes and focusing on the water drawing out negativity from your aura. Visualize the saltwater washing away any energetic debris.
3. **Speak the Spell:** Say, "Water and salt, cleanse my skin, cleanse my aura, light within."

754. Bay Leaf Aura Purge
What You Need:

- A few bay leaves (for protection and purification)
- A black pen
- A fireproof bowl

Steps:

1. **Write Intentions:** Write the word "Purify" on each bay leaf with the black pen.
2. **Burn the Leaves:** Light the bay leaves and place them in the fireproof bowl. As they burn, visualize the smoke purifying your aura.
3. **Speak the Spell:** Say, "Bay leaves burn, cleanse my space, purify my aura, grant me grace."

755. Candle Flame Aura Cleanse
What You Need:

- A white candle (for purity)
- Rosemary oil

Steps:

1. **Anoint the Candle:** Rub a small amount of rosemary oil onto the candle, focusing on its purifying energy.
2. **Light the Candle:** Light the candle and place it in front of you. Sit comfortably and gaze at the flame, allowing its light to fill your aura with purifying energy.

3. **Speak the Spell:** Say, "Candle bright, flame so pure, cleanse my aura, strong and sure."

756. Moonlight Energy Refill
What You Need:

- A small bowl of water
- A few drops of lavender oil

Steps:

1. **Prepare the Bowl:** Place the water in a small bowl and add the lavender oil.
2. **Charge Under Moonlight:** Place the bowl outside under the light of the full moon to absorb its cleansing energy.
3. **Anoint Yourself:** Use the moon-charged water to anoint your forehead and heart, saying, "Moonlight bright, fill my soul, cleanse my energy, make me whole."

757. Herb Sachet Energy Shield
What You Need:

- A small sachet
- Dried rosemary (for protection)
- Dried sage (for purification)
- A piece of clear quartz

Steps:

1. **Fill the Sachet:** Place the rosemary, sage, and clear quartz into the sachet, focusing on their protective and purifying properties.
2. **Seal the Energy:** Say, "Herbs of strength, crystal clear, shield my energy, keep it near."

3. **Carry the Sachet:** Keep the sachet with you to maintain a cleansed and protected aura throughout the day.

758. Pine Needle Aura Sweep
What You Need:

- A bundle of dried pine needles (for grounding and cleansing)

Steps:

1. **Sweep Your Aura:** Use the bundle of pine needles to gently "sweep" around your body, starting from your head and moving downward to your feet.
2. **Visualize:** Visualize the pine needles brushing away negative energy from your aura.

759. Rosemary Smoke Clearing
What You Need:

- Dried rosemary
- A fireproof bowl

Steps:

1. **Light the Rosemary:** Place the rosemary in the bowl and light it, allowing it to smolder and produce smoke.
2. **Pass Through Smoke:** Slowly pass the smoke around your body, focusing on its cleansing properties.

760. Knot of Energy Renewal
What You Need:

• A piece of white ribbon

Steps:

1. **Tie Nine Knots:** As you tie each knot, focus on your intention to renew your energy and cleanse your aura.
2. **Wear the Ribbon:** Carry or wear the knotted ribbon, saying, "Knot of light, cleanse my space, renew my aura, bring me grace."

761-800. Additional Energy Cleansing Spells
Here are more spells for energy cleansing using the transformative power of Samhain:

761. Salt Circle – Stand in a circle of sea salt, visualizing it drawing out negativity from your aura.

762. Lavender Mist – Mix lavender oil with water, spray it around your body to cleanse your energy.

763. Sage and Saltwater – Anoint your hands with sage-infused saltwater for purification.

764. Bay Leaf Anointing – Write "Cleanse" on a bay leaf, burn it in a flame.

765. Amethyst Aura Sweep – Hold an amethyst crystal, move it around your body to cleanse your energy.

766. Crystal Grid – Arrange clear quartz and amethyst in a grid around you for energy restoration.

767. Candle Flame Meditation – Light a white candle and focus on its flame purifying your aura.

768. Herb Knotting – Knot rosemary and sage into a cloth, carry it for continuous cleansing.

769. Salt and Rosemary Bath – Add salt and rosemary to your bathwater to cleanse your aura.

770. Moon Water Wash – Use moon-charged water to wash your face, clearing your energy.

771. Bay Leaf Charm – Create a charm bag with bay leaves, carry it for ongoing protection.

772. Sunlight Cleansing – Stand in sunlight, visualizing it purifying your aura.

773. Lavender Pillow – Place dried lavender under your pillow for energy renewal.

774. Salt Jar – Keep a jar of sea salt in your room to absorb negative energy.

775. Pinecone Charm – Carry a pinecone with you for grounding and energy balance.

776. Morning Dew Blessing – Anoint your forehead with morning dew for clarity.

777. Crystal Knot – Tie a knot in a ribbon around a crystal for personal protection.

778. Sunflower Seed Bath – Add sunflower seeds to your bath for energy restoration.

779. Candle Wax Seal – Drip wax onto a piece of paper, visualizing it absorbing your negativity.

780. Knot of Purity – Tie a white ribbon, focusing on purifying your energy.

781. Bay Leaf Circle – Place bay leaves in a circle around your space for energy clearing.

782. Pine Needle Sachet – Create a sachet with pine needles for grounding.

783. Rosemary Knotting – Knot rosemary into a cloth, hang it in your room.

784. Saltwater Anointing – Anoint your hands with saltwater to cleanse energy.

785. Amethyst Circle – Place amethyst stones around you for aura restoration.

786. Lavender Smoke – Burn lavender, passing its smoke through your aura.

787. Rose Water Bath – Add rose petals to your bath for energy renewal.

788. Candle Flame Anointing – Light a candle, focusing on its energy clearing your aura.

789. Crystal Bath – Place crystals in your bathwater for cleansing.

790. Herb Anointing – Rub sage oil on your temples for purification.

791. Knot of Light – Tie a white ribbon around your wrist for ongoing energy cleansing.

792. Lavender Water Spray – Create a lavender spray for energy clearing.

793. Moonlight Meditation – Meditate under moonlight to cleanse your aura.

794. Crystal Light Bath – Use selenite during a bath for spiritual cleansing.

795. Morning Sun Ritual – Stand in sunlight, focusing on its warmth clearing your aura.

796. Rosemary Circle – Create a circle of rosemary around you for energy protection.

797. Candle Meditation – Focus on a candle flame for energy clearing.

798. Saltwater Circle – Stand in a circle of salt for personal purification.

799. Herb Knot – Tie knots in a ribbon with herbs for cleansing.

800. Crystal Grid – Create a grid around your bed with cleansing crystals.

These energy cleansing spells tap into the power of Samhain and the natural world to purify your aura and elevate your spiritual vibrational state. By incorporating elements like herbs, crystals, water, and light, these rituals help you maintain an aura free from negativity and full of vibrant, positive energy. Use these spells whenever you feel the need to clear away energetic debris and restore inner balance.

Part V: Divination and Psychic Spells (801-900)

Chapter 22: Divination Spells (801-850): Spells to Enhance Tarot, Runes, and Other Divination Practices

Samhain is known as the "Witch's New Year," a time when the veil between the physical world and the spirit realm is at its thinnest, making it a powerful period for divination practices. This is the ideal time to enhance your abilities with tarot, runes, scrying, and other forms of spiritual guidance. The following spells are designed to deepen your connection to the mystical realms, sharpen your intuition, and strengthen your divination skills.

From scrying in pumpkin water to opening your third eye, these spells draw on the ancient energy of Samhain to help you receive messages from the universe, gain clarity, and tap into hidden knowledge. This chapter includes the "Pumpkin Scrying Ritual" and "Third Eye Awakening," followed by an array of spells to support your divination practices and rituals.

801. Pumpkin Scrying Ritual

The "Pumpkin Scrying Ritual" uses the essence of a pumpkin—a symbol of abundance, protection, and insight—to create a scrying vessel that enhances your ability to receive visions and messages from the spirit realm.

What You Need:

- A small pumpkin
- A carving knife
- A black candle (for focus and spiritual guidance)
- A bowl of water
- A pinch of sea salt (for purification)
- A quiet, dimly lit space

Steps:

1. **Prepare the Pumpkin:** Carve the top off the pumpkin and scoop out the seeds, leaving the interior smooth and hollow. As you do this, focus on your intention to create a sacred scrying vessel that will help you connect with the spiritual realm.

2. **Create the Scrying Water:** Fill a bowl with water and add a pinch of sea salt, stirring gently to purify the water. Pour the water into the hollow pumpkin, visualizing it becoming a reflective portal that will reveal hidden truths.

3. **Set Up Your Space:** Place the pumpkin on a table or altar in front of you. Light the black candle and place it beside the pumpkin to create a mystical ambiance. Dim the lights or perform this ritual by candlelight to enhance your focus.

4. **Begin the Scrying:** Sit comfortably and gaze into the water inside the pumpkin. Relax your eyes and mind, allowing your focus to soften. As you stare into the water, breathe deeply and evenly, opening yourself to any images, symbols, or visions that may appear.

5. **Speak the Incantation:** Whisper softly, "Pumpkin vessel, dark and deep, show me visions, secrets keep. Veil is thin, spirits near, bring me knowledge, make it clear."

6. **Receive Messages:** Continue gazing into the water, staying open to whatever impressions come to you. Trust your intuition and let the images or feelings flow naturally. If you see symbols, take note of them as they may have specific meanings related to your query.

7. **Close the Ritual:** When you feel ready to end the scrying, thank the spirits or energies that aided you. Blow out the candle and pour the water from the pumpkin back into the earth as an offering, sealing the ritual.

802. Third Eye Awakening

The "Third Eye Awakening" spell aims to open and enhance your third eye chakra, the center of intuition and inner vision. This spell helps you access deeper insights and strengthens your ability to connect with spiritual guidance during divination practices.

What You Need:

- A small amethyst crystal (for enhancing intuition)
- A piece of lavender (for spiritual clarity)
- A purple candle (for third eye activation)
- A few drops of sandalwood oil (for spiritual connection)

Steps:

1. **Set Up Your Space:** Find a quiet place where you can sit comfortably. Place the amethyst, lavender, and candle on a small table or altar in front of you. Anoint the candle with a few drops of sandalwood oil, focusing on its purpose to awaken your third eye.
2. **Light the Candle:** Light the purple candle, allowing its flame to focus your mind and connect you with higher spiritual energies.
3. **Hold the Amethyst:** Pick up the amethyst crystal and hold it against your forehead, at the point of your third eye. Close your eyes and take several deep breaths to center yourself.
4. **Visualize the Opening:** As you breathe, imagine a soft, violet light radiating from the amethyst and entering your third eye. Visualize this light gently opening your third eye, clearing away any blockages and allowing your intuition to flow freely.
5. **Speak the Spell:** Chant softly, "Third eye open, sight be clear, visions come, let me hear. Amethyst bright, guide my sight, awaken now, bring me light."
6. **Meditate:** Continue holding the amethyst to your forehead while focusing on your breathing. Allow yourself to be in this meditative state for several minutes, feeling your third eye growing more receptive to spiritual insights.
7. **Close the Ritual:** When you're ready, place the amethyst on your altar as a reminder of your intention. Extinguish the candle and take a moment to ground yourself before ending the spell.

803. Tarot Card Blessing
What You Need:

- A small bowl of saltwater (for cleansing)
- A white candle (for clarity)
- Your tarot deck

Steps:

1. **Cleanse the Deck:** Light the candle and dip your fingers into the saltwater. Sprinkle a few drops of the water onto the tarot deck to cleanse it of any lingering energies.
2. **Speak the Spell:** Say, "Cards of light, cards of fate, reveal the truth, make my path straight."
3. **Shuffle:** Shuffle the deck three times, focusing on your intention for clear and truthful readings.

804. Rune Empowerment
What You Need:

- Your rune set
- A purple cloth (for spiritual insight)
- A piece of clear quartz

Steps:

1. **Lay the Cloth:** Spread the purple cloth on your altar or workspace, placing the runes on it.
2. **Charge the Runes:** Hold the clear quartz in your hand and pass it over the runes, focusing on transferring the crystal's energy to them.
3. **Speak the Spell:** Say, "Runes of wisdom, symbols of might, grant me vision, reveal what's right."

805. Candle Divination Focus
What You Need:

- A black candle (for insight into the unknown)

Steps:

1. **Light the Candle:** Place the candle in front of you and light it, focusing on the flame.
2. **Gaze into the Flame:** Allow your eyes to relax as you gaze into the candle's flame, opening your mind to receive insights.
3. **Speak the Spell:** Say, "Flame of night, show me sight, reveal the truth, guide my light."

806. Moon Water Divination
What You Need:

- A small bowl of water
- A clear quartz crystal
- Moonlight (best during a full moon)

Steps:

1. **Create the Moon Water:** Place the bowl of water outside under the light of the full moon, with the quartz crystal beside it to charge the water.
2. **Use for Divination:** During your divination session, anoint your third eye and hands with the moon water to enhance your intuitive abilities.

807. Divination Circle Protection
What You Need:

- Sea salt
- Dried rosemary (for protection)

Steps:

1. **Create the Circle:** Sprinkle the sea salt and rosemary in a circle around your divination space.
2. **Speak the Spell:** Say, "Circle of salt, rosemary true, guard this space, bring clear view."

808. Lavender Insight Oil
What You Need:

- A small bottle of lavender oil
- A piece of amethyst

Steps:

1. **Charge the Oil:** Hold the lavender oil and the amethyst in your hands, focusing on their energies enhancing your intuition.
2. **Anoint Before Divination:** Rub a drop of lavender oil on your third eye before beginning your divination session.

809. Pendulum Clarity Spell
What You Need:

- Your pendulum
- A small bowl of saltwater

Steps:

1. **Cleanse the Pendulum:** Dip the pendulum into the saltwater, saying, "Water pure, salt so bright, cleanse this pendulum, bring true sight."
2. **Charge:** Hold the pendulum in your hands and visualize it glowing with clear, bright light.

810. Tarot Spread Enhancement
What You Need:

- A candle (white for clarity)
- Your tarot deck

Steps:

1. **Light the Candle:** Light the candle and place it near your tarot spread.
2. **Speak the Spell:** Say, "Cards of fate, show me clear, reveal the truth, bring answers near."

811-850. Additional Divination Spells
Here are more spells to enhance your divination practices using Samhain's mystical energy:

811. Amethyst Meditation – Hold an amethyst crystal to your third eye during meditation to enhance visions.

812. Bay Leaf Burn – Write "Clarity" on a bay leaf and burn it before divination to clear your mind.

813. Salt Circle – Stand in a circle of salt before scrying for protection and focus.

814. Crystal Grid – Create a grid with amethyst and clear quartz around your tarot deck to enhance its energy.

815. Candle Scrying – Gaze into a black candle's flame to open your mind to spiritual insights.

816. Moonstone Charm – Carry a moonstone in your pocket during divination for enhanced intuition.

817. Herb Sachet – Create a sachet with lavender and rosemary, place it near your divination tools.

818. Knot of Clarity – Tie nine knots in a purple ribbon, focusing on clarity and insight.

819. Rosemary Tea – Brew rosemary tea and sip it before divination to enhance your spiritual awareness.

820. Lavender Water – Spray lavender-infused water around your workspace to clear stagnant energy.

821. Clear Quartz Cleanse – Place a piece of clear quartz on your tarot deck overnight to cleanse and charge it.

822. Candlelight Focus – Meditate by candlelight to sharpen your focus before reading runes or cards.

823. Amethyst Bath – Take a bath with an amethyst crystal to clear your energy field.

824. Bay Leaf Blessing – Place a bay leaf on your tarot cards for protection and clarity.

825. Salt and Sage Smudge – Smudge your divination tools with sage smoke to clear any residual energies.

826. Moon Water Anointing – Anoint your third eye with moon-charged water for enhanced intuition.

827. Crystal Circle – Arrange crystals in a circle around your scrying bowl for focused energy.

828. Apple Blossom Oil – Anoint your tarot cards with apple blossom oil for insight and truth.

829. Morning Dew Wash – Wash your hands with morning dew before performing divination.

830. Knot of Insight – Tie a knot in a white ribbon for spiritual clarity.

831. Candle Meditation – Gaze into a candle flame to open your inner vision.

832. Sunlight Blessing – Place your tarot cards in sunlight to cleanse and recharge them.

833. Crystal Bath – Place crystals in your bathwater to cleanse your aura before divination.

834. Moon Meditation – Meditate under the moonlight to connect with its guidance.

835. Herb Pouch – Carry a pouch with rosemary and lavender for enhanced intuition.

836. Clear Quartz Anointing – Anoint your third eye with clear quartz for clear vision.

837. Saltwater Circle – Create a circle with saltwater around your tarot spread for protection.

838. Candlelight Circle – Sit in a circle of candles for focused meditation.

839. Knot of Focus – Tie knots in a purple ribbon for spiritual focus.

840. Apple Seed Spell – Place apple seeds on your altar for wisdom and guidance.

841. Lavender Pillow – Sleep with lavender under your pillow for enhanced dream divination.

842. Crystal Spray – Create a crystal-infused spray for your divination space.

843. Candle Anointing – Anoint a candle with lavender oil before divination.

844. Moonstone Meditation – Meditate with a moonstone for inner guidance.

845. Herb Knot – Knot herbs into a sachet for focused energy.

846. Salt Circle Cleansing – Create a salt circle to cleanse your divination tools.

847. Bay Leaf Scrying – Place bay leaves in your scrying bowl for clarity.

848. Knot of Light – Tie a ribbon around your tarot cards for truth.

849. Candle Scrying – Use candlelight to scry for visions.

850. Clear Quartz Meditation – Hold a clear quartz while meditating for clear insight.

These divination spells harness Samhain's mystical energies to enhance your spiritual practices, deepen your intuition, and connect with the unseen realms. By using elements like herbs, crystals, candles, and the moon's light, these spells help you access deeper wisdom and clarity in your divination work. Use these rituals to receive guidance, strengthen your psychic abilities, and explore the mysteries of the universe.

Chapter 23: Psychic Power Spells (851-900): Spells to Enhance Psychic Abilities

Samhain is a time of powerful magic, introspection, and heightened spiritual awareness. During this period, the veil between the physical and spiritual realms is at its thinnest, making it an ideal time to work on developing and enhancing psychic abilities. Whether you want to strengthen your intuition, open your third eye, or deepen your connection to the spiritual realm, these spells can aid in awakening and amplifying your psychic powers.

This chapter includes spells designed to awaken and enhance various psychic abilities, including clairvoyance, clairaudience, telepathy, and intuitive insight. The use of natural elements, crystals, herbs, and the energies of Samhain will help to open your mind and heighten your senses. We begin with the "Samhain Intuition Boost" and "Mystic Sight Spell," then delve into additional spells to further refine your psychic gifts.

851. Samhain Intuition Boost

The "Samhain Intuition Boost" spell is designed to enhance your natural intuition, tapping into the heightened spiritual energy of Samhain to unlock deeper insights and subconscious wisdom. This spell uses the powerful symbolism of apples, a fruit of wisdom and inner knowledge often associated with Samhain.

What You Need:

- A fresh apple
- A purple candle (for psychic energy)
- A small bowl of water (for clarity)
- A sprig of rosemary (for mental clarity)
- A quiet space for meditation

Steps:

1. **Prepare Your Space:** Find a quiet, dimly lit area where you can perform this spell without interruptions. Set up a small altar or table with the apple, candle, bowl of water, and rosemary. Light the purple candle to represent your intention to heighten your intuition.
2. **Create the Psychic Connection:** Hold the apple in your hands and close your eyes. Take a few deep breaths to center yourself. Visualize the apple as a source of ancient wisdom and psychic insight. Imagine its energy merging with your own, enhancing your intuitive abilities.
3. **Focus on the Water:** Place the apple in the bowl of water, allowing it to float. This represents the fluidity and clarity of psychic perception. Sprinkle the rosemary into the water, focusing on its properties for mental clarity and heightened awareness.
4. **Speak the Incantation:** Say, "Apple of wisdom, knowledge so deep, open my mind, let insights seep. Water so clear, guide my sight, boost intuition, grant me light."
5. **Meditate:** Gaze into the water, allowing your mind to drift. Take slow, deep breaths as you open yourself to the energies around you. Feel your intuition growing stronger, more perceptive, and clear.
6. **Close the Ritual:** When you feel ready, blow out the candle and remove the apple from the water. You can eat the apple later to internalize the energies, or you can bury it in the earth as an offering to the spirits for aiding your psychic growth.

852. Mystic Sight Spell

The "Mystic Sight Spell" focuses on enhancing your clairvoyant abilities, allowing you to see beyond the physical realm. This spell uses the properties of crystals and herbs to activate your third eye and improve your psychic sight.

What You Need:

- A small amethyst crystal (for intuition and third eye activation)
- A piece of bay leaf (for psychic vision)
- A purple ribbon (for spiritual focus)
- A small vial of lavender oil (for spiritual clarity)

Steps:

1. **Prepare the Crystal:** Hold the amethyst in your hands and close your eyes. Visualize a violet light radiating from the crystal, filling your mind with clarity and opening your psychic sight.
2. **Create the Charm:** Place the amethyst and bay leaf together and wrap them with the purple ribbon to form a small bundle. As you do this, focus on the intention to enhance your psychic vision and awareness.
3. **Anoint with Oil:** Apply a drop of lavender oil to the bundle, saying, "Lavender's bloom, open my sight, grant me vision, clear as light."
4. **Use as a Talisman:** Carry the charm with you or place it under your pillow at night to enhance your clairvoyance. Hold it during meditation to amplify your psychic visions.

853. Third Eye Candle Ritual
What You Need:

- A purple candle (for third eye activation)
- Rosemary oil (for mental clarity)

Steps:

1. **Anoint the Candle:** Rub a small amount of rosemary oil onto the candle while focusing on your intention to open and enhance your third eye.
2. **Light the Candle:** Place the candle in front of you and light it, gazing into the flame as you meditate.
3. **Speak the Spell:** Say, "Flame of purple, light so clear, open my mind, let visions appear."

854. Psychic Shielding Spell
What You Need:

- A small piece of hematite (for grounding and protection)
- A white candle (for purity and focus)

Steps:

1. **Hold the Hematite:** Sit in a quiet place and hold the hematite in your hands. Visualize it forming a protective shield around your aura, filtering out any distracting or negative energies.
2. **Light the Candle:** Light the white candle to represent clarity and psychic purity.
3. **Speak the Spell:** Say, "Hematite strong, shield of light, guard my mind, enhance my sight."

855. Lavender Dream Enhancement
What You Need:

- Dried lavender (for calm and spiritual clarity)
- A sachet

Steps:

1. **Fill the Sachet:** Place the dried lavender into the sachet, focusing on its properties to enhance dreams and intuitive messages.
2. **Place Under Pillow:** Put the sachet under your pillow to receive clearer dreams and messages from your subconscious.

856. Crystal Telepathy Spell
What You Need:

- Clear quartz crystal (for amplifying psychic energy)

Steps:

1. **Hold the Crystal:** Sit comfortably and hold the clear quartz in your hands. Close your eyes and focus on your intention to enhance your telepathic abilities.
2. **Visualize Connection:** Picture a beam of light extending from your third eye to another person, forming a bridge for thoughts and feelings.
3. **Speak the Spell:** Say, "Quartz so clear, amplify, connect my mind, thoughts to fly."

857. Rosemary Smoke Aura Cleanse
What You Need:

- Dried rosemary
- A fireproof bowl

Steps:

1. **Light the Rosemary:** Burn the rosemary in the fireproof bowl, allowing the smoke to fill the air around you.
2. **Cleanse Your Aura:** Pass the smoke around your body, visualizing it clearing your aura to sharpen your psychic senses.
3. **Speak the Spell:** Say, "Smoke of rosemary, cleanse my mind, open my sight, make it refined."

858. Moonstone Clairvoyance Ritual
What You Need:

- A piece of moonstone (for psychic awareness)
- A small bowl of water

Steps:

1. **Charge the Moonstone:** Place the moonstone in the bowl of water. Leave it outside under the moonlight overnight to charge.
2. **Use in Meditation:** Hold the moonstone during meditation to enhance your clairvoyant abilities.

859. Candlelight Intuition Meditation
What You Need:

- A blue candle (for intuition)
- A quiet space

Steps:

1. **Light the Candle:** Light the blue candle and sit comfortably in front of it. Focus on its flame, allowing your mind to become still.
2. **Speak the Spell:** Say, "Candle of blue, clear my mind, open my sight, wisdom find."

860. Saltwater Anointing

What You Need:

- Sea salt
- A small bowl of water

Steps:

1. **Create the Mixture:** Dissolve the sea salt into the water, focusing on its purifying and grounding properties.
2. **Anoint Your Forehead:** Dip your finger into the saltwater and anoint your third eye, saying, "Salt and water, pure and true, open my sight, clear my view."

861-900. Additional Psychic Power Spells

Here are additional spells to enhance your psychic abilities using Samhain's mystical energy:

861. Amethyst Meditation – Meditate while holding an amethyst crystal to open your psychic channels.

862. Bay Leaf Scrying – Place a bay leaf under your pillow to receive psychic visions in your dreams.

863. Candle Gazing – Gaze into a candle flame to practice strengthening your focus and intuition.

864. Clear Quartz Circle – Create a circle with clear quartz crystals to amplify your psychic power.

865. Herb Sachet – Create a sachet with rosemary and lavender for intuitive clarity.

866. Lavender Oil Anointing – Anoint your third eye with lavender oil to enhance psychic awareness.

867. Moon Bath – Bathe in moonlight to cleanse and recharge your psychic energy.

868. Morning Dew Blessing – Anoint your forehead with morning dew for fresh psychic insight.

869. Knot of Clarity – Tie nine knots in a purple ribbon to focus your psychic energy.

870. Candlelight Focus – Meditate by candlelight to enhance your inner vision.

871. Crystal Grid – Arrange a crystal grid with amethyst and clear quartz around you.

872. Rosemary Smoke – Smudge your space with rosemary to clear away energetic blocks.

873. Salt Circle – Stand in a circle of salt before psychic work for protection and focus.

874. Moon Water Anointing – Anoint your hands with moon-charged water before divination.

875. Apple Blossom Oil – Anoint your temples with apple blossom oil to open your psychic senses.

876. Herb Knotting – Knot herbs into a sachet and hang it near your bed.

877. Crystal Bath – Add crystals to your bathwater to cleanse your energy.

878. Candle Scrying – Gaze into a candle flame to practice seeing beyond the physical realm.

879. Lavender Pillow – Sleep with lavender under your pillow to enhance intuitive dreams.

880. Sunlight Blessing – Stand in sunlight, focusing on its energy to open your psychic sight.

881. Bay Leaf Charm – Place a bay leaf in your pocket to carry psychic protection.

882. Amethyst Anointing – Anoint your third eye with an amethyst to activate your inner vision.

883. Knot of Focus – Tie a white ribbon around your wrist for focused psychic work.

884. Saltwater Bath – Soak in a saltwater bath to clear your energy field.

885. Crystal Light Meditation – Meditate with a piece of selenite to cleanse and heighten your psychic awareness.

886. Candle of Sight – Light a purple candle to illuminate your psychic path.

887. Lavender Smoke – Burn lavender to cleanse your aura and enhance intuition.

888. Rose Quartz Anointing – Rub rose quartz on your temples for emotional clarity.

889. Clear Quartz Amplification – Hold a clear quartz while focusing on amplifying your psychic abilities.

890. Crystal Knot – Tie a crystal into a ribbon for ongoing psychic support.

891. Candlelight Meditation – Gaze into a candle flame to open your psychic channels.

892. Bay Leaf Burn – Write "Psychic Power" on a bay leaf, burn it for enhancement.

893. Herb Pouch – Carry a pouch with lavender and rosemary for psychic clarity.

894. Moon Meditation – Meditate under moonlight to heighten your psychic senses.

895. Crystal Aura Sweep – Sweep a selenite wand through your aura for energetic cleansing.

896. Apple Seed Spell – Carry apple seeds for wisdom and psychic growth.

897. Candle Anointing – Anoint a candle with lavender oil for psychic focus.

898. Herb Knotting – Knot herbs into a cloth for clarity.

899. Moon Water Cleanse – Wash your hands with moon-charged water before divination.

900. Clear Quartz Meditation – Hold a clear quartz during meditation to open your psychic channels.

These psychic power spells harness the potent energies of Samhain to enhance your intuitive abilities, sharpen your inner sight, and open your mind to spiritual guidance. Using elements like herbs, crystals, candlelight, and moonlight, these spells provide pathways for developing and amplifying your psychic gifts. Perform these rituals when you seek to deepen your connection with the spiritual realm and access the hidden truths of the universe.

Part VI: Transformation Spells (901-1000)

Chapter 24: Personal Transformation Spells (901-950): Spells for Self-Growth and Change

Samhain is a time of endings and beginnings, making it the perfect occasion for personal transformation. As the wheel of the year turns, Samhain marks the closing of one chapter and the initiation of another, inviting us to release what no longer serves us and embrace new aspects of ourselves. The spells in this chapter are designed to aid in personal transformation, guiding you toward self-growth, empowerment, and inner change.

From embracing new habits to shedding old patterns, these rituals help harness the energy of the season to facilitate deep, personal metamorphosis. The "Samhain Renewal Rite" and "Autumn Phoenix Rebirth" are just the beginning of a collection of spells intended to help you navigate your journey of self-growth and transformation.

901. Samhain Renewal Rite

The "Samhain Renewal Rite" is a spell designed to clear away old energies, behaviors, or habits and make room for new growth. By releasing the past, this spell harnesses the power of Samhain to open you up to new opportunities and personal renewal.

What You Need:

- A black candle (for banishing the old)
- A white candle (for new beginnings)
- A piece of paper and pen
- A small bowl
- A pinch of dried rosemary (for mental clarity and protection)
- A lighter or matches

Steps:

1. **Prepare Your Space:** Find a quiet space where you can perform this spell without interruption. Set up the black candle on your left and the white candle on your right, with the paper and bowl in front of you.

2. **Write What You Wish to Release:** Take the piece of paper and write down any habits, patterns, or aspects of yourself that you wish to release. Be honest with yourself, and let the words flow freely.

3. **Anoint the Candles:** Anoint the black candle with the dried rosemary to symbolize the clearing of old energies. Light the black candle first, saying, "Flame of night, burn away. Release the old, make room for day."

4. **Burn the Paper:** Hold the piece of paper in your hands and focus on your intention to let go of the things you've written. Pass the paper through the flame of the black candle, allowing it to catch fire. Drop the burning paper into the bowl, saying, "By this fire, I release. The old shall burn, my soul finds peace."

5. **Light the White Candle:** Now, light the white candle, representing new beginnings and renewal. As you light it, say, "Flame of white, pure and bright. Bring me change, new path in sight."

6. **Visualize the Transformation:** Spend a few moments gazing into the flame of the white candle, visualizing yourself transformed—free from the burdens you released and embracing the new qualities you wish to embody.

7. **Close the Ritual:** When you're ready, extinguish both candles. Scatter the ashes from the bowl outdoors, symbolizing the final release of the old energy. Keep the white candle to light whenever you need a reminder of your renewed path.

902. Autumn Phoenix Rebirth

The "Autumn Phoenix Rebirth" spell taps into the mythological energy of the phoenix, a creature that is reborn from its ashes. This spell helps you embrace change, shed old skin, and experience a personal rebirth, allowing you to emerge stronger and more vibrant.

What You Need:

- A small bowl of ashes (collected from a previous ritual or burned herbs)
- A feather (to represent the phoenix)
- A red candle (for transformation and passion)
- A piece of red ribbon

- A quiet outdoor space

Steps:

1. **Find Your Space:** Go to a quiet, outdoor space where you won't be disturbed. Light the red candle and place it in front of you.
2. **Hold the Feather:** Take the feather in your hands and close your eyes. Imagine yourself as a phoenix, shedding the old layers of your being and preparing for rebirth.
3. **Sprinkle the Ashes:** Hold the bowl of ashes and sprinkle a small amount on the ground around the candle, saying, "From these ashes, I shall rise. Shed the old, birth the wise."
4. **Tie the Ribbon:** Wrap the red ribbon around the feather while focusing on the qualities you wish to embrace in your rebirth. Visualize yourself transformed, filled with new energy, strength, and passion.
5. **Speak the Incantation:** Say, "Like the phoenix, I renew. From the old, I emerge true. Flames of change, burn so bright. Bring me strength, ignite my light."
6. **Close the Spell:** Blow out the candle and keep the feather as a symbol of your rebirth. Place it on your altar or in a safe space to remind you of your transformation journey.

903. Harvest of Self-Growth
What You Need:

- A small pumpkin (to symbolize harvest and growth)
- A green candle (for personal growth)
- A pen and small piece of paper
- A carving knife

Steps:

1. **Carve the Pumpkin:** Cut the top off the pumpkin and hollow it out, setting the seeds aside. As you do this, focus on removing old habits and making room for growth.

2. **Write Your Intentions:** Write what you wish to cultivate in yourself on the piece of paper.
3. **Place Inside the Pumpkin:** Place the paper inside the pumpkin and light the green candle next to it, saying, "Seed of growth, pumpkin bright, bring me change, new insight."

904. Candle of Confidence
What You Need:

- A yellow candle (for confidence and self-empowerment)
- A small bottle of rosemary oil (for mental clarity)

Steps:

1. **Anoint the Candle:** Rub the rosemary oil onto the candle, focusing on the intention of building your confidence.
2. **Light the Candle:** Light the candle and sit in front of it, visualizing yourself filled with radiant confidence and self-assurance.
3. **Speak the Spell:** Say, "Flame of yellow, bold and bright, grant me strength, fill me with light."

905. Knot of Transformation
What You Need:

- A piece of black ribbon (for releasing the old)
- A piece of white ribbon (for embracing the new)

Steps:

1. **Tie the Knots:** Begin by tying knots in the black ribbon, each representing something you wish to let go of.
2. **Speak the Spell:** Say, "Knots of black, hold the past, release to change, freedom at last."

3. **Tie the White Ribbon:** Tie knots in the white ribbon, each representing a quality you wish to embrace.

906. Mirror of Self-Acceptance
What You Need:

- A small hand mirror
- A pink candle (for self-love)
- Rose oil (for emotional healing)

Steps:

1. **Anoint the Mirror:** Rub a drop of rose oil onto the mirror.
2. **Light the Candle:** Place the mirror in front of the pink candle and light it.
3. **Speak the Spell:** Look into the mirror and say, "Reflection true, I now see, love and strength reside in me."

907. Morning Dew Renewal
What You Need:

- A small container to collect morning dew
- A green ribbon

Steps:

1. **Collect Dew:** Go outside at dawn and collect morning dew in the container.
2. **Anoint Yourself:** Dip your fingers into the dew and touch your forehead and heart, saying, "Dew of dawn, fresh and bright, renew my soul, grant me light."

908. Crystal of Transformation
What You Need:

- A piece of clear quartz (for amplification)
- A black candle

Steps:

1. **Light the Candle:** Light the black candle to symbolize the release of old energy.
2. **Hold the Crystal:** Hold the quartz and visualize it absorbing the old, stagnant energy.
3. **Speak the Spell:** Say, "Quartz of light, amplify, cleanse the old, let it fly."

909. Lavender Self-Love Bath
What You Need:

- A handful of dried lavender (for calm and self-love)
- A handful of sea salt

Steps:

1. **Prepare the Bath:** Add the lavender and salt to the bathwater.
2. **Soak:** Enter the bath and visualize the water infusing you with self-love and strength.
3. **Speak the Spell:** Say, "Water calm, lavender bright, fill me with love, grant me light."

910. Herbal Renewal Sachet
What You Need:

- A small sachet
- Dried rosemary (for mental clarity)
- Dried lavender (for self-love)
- A small piece of clear quartz

Steps:

1. **Fill the Sachet:** Place the herbs and quartz into the sachet, focusing on renewal and growth.
2. **Carry the Sachet:** Keep the sachet with you to support your transformation journey.

911-950. Additional Personal Transformation Spells

Here are more spells for personal transformation using the energy of Samhain:

911. Bay Leaf Release – Write old habits on a bay leaf, burn it for release.

912. Saltwater Anointing – Anoint your forehead with saltwater for renewal.

913. Crystal Circle – Create a circle of clear quartz crystals to amplify change.

914. Candle of Courage – Light a red candle to fill you with courage.

915. Herb Knotting – Knot herbs into a ribbon to symbolize change.

916. Knot of Strength – Use a piece of purple ribbon to tie knots for each goal you have. Each knot represents strength and commitment to your transformation.

917. Moonstone Bath – Fill your bath with moonstones and visualize their energies cleansing your aura and preparing you for transformation.

918. Mirror of Reflection – Use a mirror to reflect on your progress. Each time you look, remind yourself of the growth you've achieved.

919. Sunlight Blessing – Stand in sunlight for a few moments daily, visualizing its rays enhancing your personal growth and vitality.

920. Crystal Cleansing – Cleanse your crystals regularly in moonlight to ensure they're charged and ready to assist in your transformation.

921. Lavender Pillow – Sleep with lavender to promote restful sleep and invite dreams of personal growth.

922. Rosemary Meditation – Incorporate rosemary into your meditation routine to enhance focus and clarity during your transformation journey.

923. Knot of Release – Tie knots in a ribbon as you release negative thoughts, visualizing them dissolving.

924. Amethyst Anointing – Use an amethyst crystal to anoint your third eye, enhancing your intuitive abilities and guiding you on your path.

925. Salt Circle – Create a protective circle of salt around your space to enhance focus and keep distractions at bay during your rituals.

926. Candlelight Meditation – Utilize candlelight to foster a meditative environment that supports transformation.

927. Herb Pouch – Carry a pouch filled with transformation-focused herbs to keep your intentions close to your heart.

928. Morning Dew Blessing – Collect morning dew, and use it to anoint yourself with the intention of fresh beginnings each day.

929. Crystal Bath – Add crystals like rose quartz to your bath for emotional healing and self-love.

930. Knot of Focus – Tie a knot in a white ribbon to symbolize your commitment to staying focused on your goals.

931. Moon Water Ritual – Use moon-charged water in your rituals to enhance intentions of transformation.

932. Lavender Meditation – Incorporate lavender into your meditation to promote relaxation and emotional balance.

933. Crystal Light Bath – Soak in a bath filled with crystals to absorb their energy and enhance your personal transformation.

934. Saltwater Circle – Create a circle with saltwater to protect your energy while focusing on personal growth.

935. Candle of Reflection – Use a candle to focus on personal growth and progress, speaking your intentions aloud.

936. Bay Leaf Scrying – Use bay leaves in a scrying bowl for insights into your transformation journey.

937. Amethyst Cleansing – Use an amethyst crystal to cleanse your aura and invite clarity.

938. Knot of Focus – Tie a piece of ribbon for each goal you want to accomplish, visualizing success.

939. Herbal Anointing – Anoint your forehead with herbs for clarity and transformation.

940. Crystal Grid – Set up a crystal grid around your workspace to amplify energies related to growth and transformation.

941. Lavender Infusion – Infuse your space with lavender to promote a sense of calm and facilitate personal growth.

942. Moonlight Meditation – Meditate in moonlight to connect with the energies of transformation and rebirth.

943. Morning Ritual – Start your day with affirmations focusing on your personal growth.

944. Salt and Rosemary Bath – Soak in a bath with salt and rosemary to cleanse your aura.

945. Candle of Reflection – Light a candle to reflect on your journey, speaking your thoughts and intentions.

946. Bay Leaf Scrying – Use bay leaves in scrying to gain insight into your personal transformation.

947. Knot of Empowerment – Tie knots in a ribbon to symbolize personal empowerment.

948. Herbal Circle – Create a circle of herbs around your sacred space for protection and focus.

949. Amethyst Meditation – Meditate with an amethyst to enhance clarity and emotional healing.

950. Saltwater Cleanse – Use saltwater to cleanse your energy field and invite renewal.

These personal transformation spells leverage the powerful energies of Samhain to facilitate profound self-growth and change. By working with various elements, including herbs, crystals, and candles, you can effectively navigate your journey toward self-improvement and embrace the opportunities for transformation that await you. Use these rituals and spells as tools to support your personal evolution, allowing you to become the best version of yourself as you journey through the seasons.

Chapter 25: Habit-Breaking Spells (951-975): Spells to Break Bad Habits

Samhain is a time of release, where the thinning of the veil between worlds allows us to easily shed the habits, behaviors, and patterns that no longer serve us. The power of Samhain's transformative energy is particularly potent for breaking bad habits and freeing ourselves from cycles of behavior that hinder our personal growth. This chapter provides detailed spells to help you release and break free from these patterns.

These habit-breaking spells use the natural elements, moon phases, and symbolism to help you banish old habits and pave the way for new, healthier patterns. Whether you want to quit a negative mindset, break a physical habit, or let go of emotional baggage, these spells guide you in aligning your intention with the forces of nature. The chapter starts with the "Waning Moon Release" and "Samhain Cord-Cutting" and continues with other powerful spells for breaking habits.

951. Waning Moon Release

The "Waning Moon Release" spell is designed to harness the energy of the waning moon, which is ideal for letting go and banishing unwanted habits. This spell uses the moon's diminishing light to symbolize the gradual fading of a habit until it disappears entirely.

What You Need:

- A black candle (for banishment)
- A piece of paper and a pen
- A small bowl
- Sea salt (for purification)
- A waning moon night (the best time to perform this spell)

Steps:

1. **Prepare Your Space:** Choose a quiet place where you won't be disturbed. Set up a small table or altar with the black candle in the center, and place the bowl nearby. Scatter some sea salt around the candle to create a protective circle.

2. **Set Your Intentions:** Take a moment to reflect on the habit you want to break. Visualize how your life will improve once you've let go of this behavior.
3. **Write Down the Habit:** On the piece of paper, write down the habit you wish to release. Be specific and honest about what you want to banish from your life.
4. **Light the Candle:** Light the black candle, saying, "Waning moon, as you decrease, take this habit, bring me peace. Burn away what holds me tight, release me now, free my light."
5. **Burn the Paper:** Hold the paper over the candle flame until it catches fire. Place the burning paper in the bowl and watch as it turns to ashes. Visualize the habit fading away with the smoke and transforming into positive energy.
6. **Scatter the Ashes:** Once the paper has burned completely, scatter the ashes outside in the wind, saying, "Gone with the smoke, carried by air, this habit fades, I no longer care."
7. **Close the Ritual:** Let the candle burn down safely, or extinguish it while focusing on the habit being banished from your life.

952. Samhain Cord-Cutting

The "Samhain Cord-Cutting" spell is designed to sever energetic ties to a habit or behavior that you wish to break free from. This ritual uses symbolic cord-cutting to release the hold that the habit has over you, empowering you to move forward.

What You Need:

- A black candle (for protection and banishment)
- A length of black string or cord
- A pair of scissors
- A small piece of paper and pen

Steps:

1. **Set Your Space:** Create a sacred space where you can perform the ritual undisturbed. Place the black candle in the center of your space and light it to invoke the protective energy of Samhain.

2. **Identify the Habit:** On the piece of paper, write down the habit you wish to break. Fold the paper and place it in front of the candle.

3. **Hold the Cord:** Take the black cord and hold it in your hands. Visualize it as the energetic connection between you and the habit you wish to sever.

4. **Speak the Incantation:** Say, "Cord of habit, bind so tight, I release you now, break this plight. With this cut, I set me free, no longer held, I now decree."

5. **Cut the Cord:** Use the scissors to cut the cord in half. As you do, visualize the hold of the habit breaking, its energy dissipating and freeing you.

6. **Burn the Paper:** Hold the paper over the flame of the black candle and let it burn, saying, "Samhain's flame, burn it bright, sever this habit, end its might."

7. **Close the Ritual:** Allow the candle to burn down naturally, or extinguish it with the intent of sealing the spell. Scatter the ashes of the burned paper outside.

953. Moonstone Habit Dissolution
What You Need:

- A piece of moonstone (for change and letting go)
- A black ribbon

Steps:

1. **Hold the Moonstone:** Sit in a quiet place, holding the moonstone in your hands. Close your eyes and visualize the habit dissolving.

2. **Wrap the Ribbon:** Wrap the black ribbon around the moonstone, focusing on it absorbing the energy of the habit.

3. **Bury the Stone:** Bury the moonstone outdoors, saying, "Earth, take this habit, transform its might, release me now, bring me light."

954. Lavender Habit-Soothing Bath
What You Need:

- A handful of dried lavender (for calm and release)
- Sea salt
- A bathtub filled with warm water

Steps:

1. **Prepare the Bath:** Add the dried lavender and sea salt to the warm bathwater.
2. **Soak and Release:** Step into the bath and focus on the water drawing out the energy of the habit you wish to break.
3. **Speak the Spell:** Say, "Water warm, lavender sweet, dissolve this habit, make me complete."

955. Knot-tying Habit Binding
What You Need:

- A piece of black ribbon
- A small piece of paper
- A pen

Steps:

1. **Write the Habit:** On the piece of paper, write down the habit you want to break.
2. **Wrap and Knot:** Wrap the paper in the black ribbon, tying three knots as you say, "Knot of one, I bind this hold. Knot of two, I break the mold. Knot of three, I now set free."
3. **Dispose:** Bury the knotted ribbon and paper outdoors.

956. Crystal Habit Breaker
What You Need:

- A piece of smoky quartz (for grounding and banishment)
- A small black pouch

Steps:

1. **Hold the Quartz:** Hold the smoky quartz and visualize it absorbing the energy of your habit.
2. **Seal the Habit:** Place the quartz in the black pouch, saying, "Crystal of smoke, absorb and bind, take this habit, release my mind."
3. **Bury the Pouch:** Bury the pouch under a tree, symbolizing the habit's absorption into the earth.

957. Saltwater Purification Ritual
What You Need:

- A small bowl of water
- Sea salt

Steps:

1. **Create Saltwater:** Add sea salt to the bowl of water and stir clockwise, focusing on the intention to cleanse away the habit.
2. **Anoint Yourself:** Dip your fingers into the water and touch your forehead and heart, saying, "Salt and water, pure and clear, cleanse this habit, disappear."

958. Bay Leaf Burning
What You Need:

- A bay leaf
- A pen
- A fireproof bowl

Steps:

1. **Write on the Bay Leaf:** Write the habit you want to break on the bay leaf.
2. **Burn the Leaf:** Hold the bay leaf over a flame until it catches fire. Place it in the fireproof bowl, saying, "Leaf of bay, burn so bright, take this habit, end its might."

959. Candle of Change
What You Need:

- A black candle (for banishment)
- Rosemary oil

Steps:

1. **Anoint the Candle:** Rub rosemary oil onto the candle while focusing on the habit you wish to break.
2. **Light the Candle:** Light the candle, saying, "Flame of black, burn away, end this habit, clear my way."

960. Knot of Freedom
What You Need:

- A piece of black cord

Steps:

1. **Tie the Knots:** Tie nine knots in the cord, focusing on releasing the habit with each knot.
2. **Speak the Spell:** Say, "Knots of nine, bind no more, habit broken, freedom's door."

961-975. Additional Habit-Breaking Spells

Here are additional spells for breaking habits using Samhain's transformative energy:

961. Herb Sachet Release – Create a sachet with rosemary and lavender. Place it under your pillow to absorb the habit's energy.

962. Salt Circle Cleansing – Create a circle of sea salt around you while focusing on releasing the habit.

963. Amethyst Meditation – Hold an amethyst while meditating on releasing your habit.

964. Candlelight Reflection – Light a black candle and reflect on how the habit has impacted your life, then blow out the candle to symbolize its end.

965. Bay Leaf Sachet – Create a sachet with bay leaves. Keep it near you as a reminder to break the habit.

966. Knot of Release – Tie knots in a ribbon, symbolizing the breaking of the habit.

967. Moon Bath – Bathe in moonlight to cleanse your energy of the habit.

968. Crystal Grid – Set up a grid with smoky quartz around your bed to absorb the habit's energy.

969. Lavender Pillow – Sleep with lavender under your pillow to soothe the habit's grip.

970. Knot of Strength – Tie knots in a purple ribbon, focusing on your strength to overcome the habit.

971. Candle of Willpower – Light a yellow candle to strengthen your willpower in breaking the habit.

972. Saltwater Anointing – Anoint your forehead with saltwater to cleanse and banish the habit.

973. Mirror Reflection – Look into a mirror and say, "I release you," visualizing the habit leaving your life.

974. Bay Leaf Scrying – Use bay leaves in scrying to gain insights on how to overcome the habit.

975. Candle Flame – Gaze into a candle flame, focusing on burning away the habit.

These habit-breaking spells leverage the potent energies of Samhain to help you let go of behaviors and patterns that no longer serve you. By working with elements like herbs, crystals, candlelight, and moon phases, you align your intentions with the natural cycles, allowing for a smoother process of change. Use these rituals to support your journey toward healthier, more fulfilling habits.

Chapter 26: New Beginnings Spells (976-1000): Spells to Embrace New Opportunities

As the wheel of the year turns at Samhain, it marks both an end and a beginning. This is the perfect time to release the old and welcome new opportunities, fresh starts, and personal growth. The energy of Samhain is ideal for planting the seeds of what you wish to manifest in the coming months. This chapter provides detailed spells designed to help you embrace new beginnings, set intentions, and open yourself to the possibilities that lie ahead.

These new beginnings spells use the natural elements of the season—like pumpkins, seeds, herbs, and symbols of change—to help you initiate positive transformation. The rituals encourage you to clear away the past and create space for new opportunities, whether in love, career, personal growth, or spiritual development. The chapter begins with the "Pumpkin Seed Planting Spell" and "Samhain Doorway of Change," followed by various other spells to set you on a path toward new adventures.

976. Pumpkin Seed Planting Spell

The "Pumpkin Seed Planting Spell" utilizes the symbolic act of planting seeds to represent new beginnings and future growth. By planting pumpkin seeds during Samhain, you channel the earth's energy to nurture your intentions, allowing them to grow and manifest in the months to come.

What You Need:

- A small pumpkin
- A knife
- Pumpkin seeds (from the pumpkin you carve)
- A small flower pot filled with soil
- A green candle (for growth and prosperity)
- A bowl of water

Steps:

1. **Prepare the Pumpkin:** Cut the top off the pumpkin and scoop out the seeds. As you do this, focus on releasing the old energy that you no longer need, creating space for new beginnings. Place the seeds in the bowl of water to cleanse them of past energies.

2. **Set Your Intentions:** Hold the seeds in your hands, close your eyes, and focus on the new beginnings or opportunities you wish to attract. Visualize these seeds growing into healthy, vibrant plants that represent your goals and desires flourishing.

3. **Light the Candle:** Light the green candle and place it beside the flower pot. The green candle symbolizes growth, prosperity, and the nurturing energy you wish to bring into your life.

4. **Plant the Seeds:** Take a few seeds and plant them in the soil of the flower pot. As you plant each seed, say, "Seeds of promise, seeds of light, grow my dreams with strength and might. As you sprout, so shall I, new beginnings now draw nigh."

5. **Water the Seeds:** Pour a small amount of water into the pot, nurturing the seeds. Visualize the water as the life force that will help your intentions take root and grow.

6. **Close the Ritual:** Allow the candle to burn for a few minutes as you meditate on your new beginnings. Extinguish the candle when you're ready, knowing that the seeds of your intentions are now planted in both the physical and spiritual realms.

7. **Nurture the Plant:** As you care for the seeds, watch for them to sprout and grow. This will serve as a reminder of the growth and opportunities manifesting in your life.

977. Samhain Doorway of Change

The "Samhain Doorway of Change" spell involves creating a symbolic doorway to pass through, representing the transition from the old to the new. This spell helps you consciously step into new opportunities and leave behind what no longer serves you.

What You Need:

- A black candle (to symbolize the end of old cycles)
- A white candle (to represent new beginnings)
- A small piece of paper and a pen
- A sprig of rosemary (for clarity and courage)

Steps:

1. **Create the Doorway:** Choose a doorway in your home to symbolize the passage into a new phase of your life. Place the black candle on one side of the doorway and the white candle on the other.
2. **Set Your Intentions:** On the piece of paper, write down what you are leaving behind as you step into your new beginning. Place the paper in front of the black candle.
3. **Light the Candles:** Light the black candle first, saying, "Candle of darkness, flame of old, I release the past, my story told." Then light the white candle, saying, "Candle of light, flame of new, I embrace change, my path pursue."
4. **Cross the Threshold:** Hold the sprig of rosemary in your hand and stand in front of the doorway. Take a deep breath, focus on your intentions, and step through the doorway. As you do, say, "Through this doorway, change I seek. I step into new, future unique."
5. **Close the Ritual:** Extinguish the black candle, symbolizing the end of the old. Leave the white candle burning for a few minutes to represent the new beginnings you are welcoming.
6. **Keep the Rosemary:** Place the rosemary on your altar or in a sacred space as a reminder of your commitment to embracing new opportunities.

978. New Moon Dream Manifestation

What You Need:

- A piece of moonstone (for new beginnings and intuition)
- A small bowl of water
- A green candle

Steps:

1. **Prepare the Space:** Place the moonstone in the bowl of water and set the green candle beside it.

2. **Light the Candle:** Light the candle, saying, "Candle bright, green and new, guide my dreams, make them true."
3. **Focus on Dreams:** Hold the moonstone and focus on the new opportunities you wish to manifest. Visualize them as vividly as possible.

979. Bay Leaf Wish
What You Need:

- A bay leaf
- A pen
- A green candle

Steps:

1. **Write on the Leaf:** Write your wish or new beginning on the bay leaf.
2. **Burn the Leaf:** Light the green candle and carefully burn the bay leaf in its flame, saying, "Bay leaf burn, wish take flight, bring new beginnings, day and night."

980. Crystal New Beginnings Charm
What You Need:

- A piece of clear quartz (for amplifying intentions)
- A green ribbon

Steps:

1. **Charge the Crystal:** Hold the clear quartz and focus on your new beginning, visualizing it as a bright light within the crystal.
2. **Tie the Ribbon:** Wrap the green ribbon around the crystal while saying, "Quartz of light, shine and grow, guide my path, let newness flow."

981. Candle of Opportunity
What You Need:

- A yellow candle (for joy and opportunity)
- Rosemary oil

Steps:

1. **Anoint the Candle:** Rub rosemary oil onto the candle while focusing on inviting new opportunities into your life.
2. **Light the Candle:** Light the candle, saying, "Flame of yellow, bold and bright, bring new chances, fill my sight."

982. Lavender New Path Bath
What You Need:

- A handful of dried lavender (for peace and new beginnings)
- Sea salt
- A bathtub filled with warm water

Steps:

1. **Prepare the Bath:** Add the dried lavender and sea salt to the bathwater.
2. **Soak:** Step into the bath and focus on releasing the past, allowing new paths to open.
3. **Speak the Spell:** Say, "Lavender blooms, salt so clear, wash away the old, bring new near."

983. Rosemary Purification
What You Need:

- A sprig of rosemary
- A piece of white ribbon

Steps:

1. **Hold the Rosemary:** Sit quietly and hold the rosemary, focusing on the fresh start you desire.
2. **Tie the Ribbon:** Wrap the white ribbon around the rosemary, saying, "Rosemary pure, guide my way, new beginnings, here to stay."

984. Amethyst Door of Change
What You Need:

- An amethyst crystal
- A small bowl of water

Steps:

1. **Charge the Crystal:** Place the amethyst in the bowl of water under the light of the full moon.
2. **Use for Focus:** Hold the amethyst during meditation to visualize your new beginning.

985. New Beginnings Herb Sachet
What You Need:

- A small sachet
- Dried rosemary (for clarity)
- Dried lavender (for peace)
- A small piece of clear quartz

Steps:

1. **Fill the Sachet:** Place the herbs and quartz into the sachet while focusing on your new intentions.
2. **Carry the Sachet:** Keep the sachet with you to support your journey toward new beginnings.

986. Salt Circle of New Beginnings
What You Need:

- Sea salt

Steps:

1. **Create the Circle:** Sprinkle sea salt around you in a circle, focusing on the protective and purifying energy.
2. **Speak the Spell:** Say, "Circle of salt, strong and bright, open my path, guide my sight."

987. Crystal Grid of Growth
What You Need:

- Clear quartz
- Amethyst
- Green aventurine

Steps:

1. **Create the Grid:** Arrange the crystals in a triangular pattern on your altar.
2. **Focus on Growth:** Sit in front of the grid and meditate on your new beginnings, visualizing them growing with the energy of the crystals.

988-1000. Additional New Beginnings Spells
Here are more spells to welcome new beginnings using Samhain's powerful energies:
988. Moon Bathing – Stand under the light of the new moon, focusing on drawing in its energy for a fresh start.
989. Candle Knot – Tie knots in a white ribbon while focusing on each new beginning you desire.
990. Bay Leaf Charm – Write your new intention on a bay leaf and keep it in your wallet as a charm for success.
991. Morning Dew Ritual – Collect morning dew and anoint your forehead, saying, "Dew of dawn, fresh and bright, open my path, clear my sight."
992. Crystal Cleansing – Cleanse a piece of clear quartz in moonlight to use in meditations for new beginnings.
993. Apple Blessing – Hold an apple in your hands and focus on it as a symbol of abundance. Eat it, visualizing yourself taking in new opportunities.

994. Sunlight Invocation – Stand in the sunlight and say, "Sun so bright, bring new light, guide my path, day and night."

995. Herb Infusion – Brew a tea with rosemary and drink it while focusing on new goals.

996. Morning Affirmations – Each morning, light a green candle and recite affirmations for new beginnings.

997. Saltwater Anointing – Use saltwater to anoint your hands before starting a new project.

998. Knot of Change – Tie knots in a green ribbon while visualizing new opportunities.

999. Lavender Oil Anointing – Anoint your wrists with lavender oil to calm the mind and open up to new beginnings.

1000. Candle Scrying – Gaze into a candle flame while focusing on the new paths opening up for you.

These new beginnings spells harness the transformative power of Samhain to open doors, plant seeds of intention, and invite fresh starts into your life. By working with elements such as herbs, crystals, candlelight, and moon phases, these rituals create an environment for personal growth and new opportunities. Use these spells to support your journey as you embrace the possibilities that await in the coming months.

Appendices

Appendix A: Glossary: Definitions of Key Spellcasting Terms and Concepts

This glossary provides definitions of important spellcasting terms and concepts used throughout the book. Understanding these terms is essential for practitioners, both new and experienced, as they explore the world of magic and spellwork. The definitions include descriptions of magical tools, spell components, and various energies that are often utilized in spells, rituals, and ceremonies.

Altar

A sacred space or flat surface dedicated to spiritual or magical work. An altar can hold items such as candles, crystals, herbs, and ritual tools, serving as a focal point for spellcasting and spiritual practices.

Anointing

The act of applying oil, water, or another substance to an object, body part, or space to imbue it with a specific magical intention. Anointing is commonly performed on candles, crystals, or oneself to bless, protect, or consecrate.

Astral Realm

A spiritual plane that exists beyond the physical world. It is believed to be where spirits, guides, and other entities reside, and where out-of-body experiences, astral projection, and other metaphysical activities occur.

Athame

A ritual knife used in spellwork to direct energy, cast circles, or carve symbols into candles. The athame typically has a double-edged blade and is not used for physical cutting.

Banishing

A magical act to remove, repel, or dispel negative energies, spirits, bad habits, or unwanted influences. Banishing spells often involve symbols of protection, such as black candles, salt, or herbs like sage.

Bay Leaf

A herb commonly used in spellwork for protection, wish-making, and purification. Burning a bay leaf with a written intention is a popular method for manifesting desires.

Binding

A spell used to restrict or contain energy, actions, or individuals. Binding spells are often used to prevent harmful behaviors or to protect against unwanted influences.

Candle Magic

A form of spellcasting that uses candles as the primary tool for focusing energy, intentions, and desires. The color of the candle often corresponds to the purpose of the spell, such as white for purity, black for banishing, or green for growth.

Casting a Circle

The act of creating a boundary or circle of protection before performing a ritual or spell. The circle serves as a sacred, safe space that holds energy and keeps out unwanted influences. Circles are often cast using an athame, wand, or hand gestures.

Cauldron

A small metal pot used in spellwork and rituals for burning herbs, mixing potions, or containing candle wax. The cauldron symbolizes transformation and the womb of the Goddess in some traditions.

Cleansing

The process of removing negative or stagnant energy from an object, space, or person. Cleansing methods include smudging with sage or other herbs, using saltwater, bathing in moonlight, or burning candles.

Correspondences

The associations between various magical items (such as herbs, colors, crystals, moon phases) and specific intentions or energies. For example, lavender corresponds to peace, rose quartz to love, and the color green to growth and prosperity.

Crystals

Minerals and stones that are believed to possess metaphysical properties, such as healing, protection, or energy amplification. Each type of crystal has its own unique vibration and corresponds to specific intentions, like amethyst for intuition or clear quartz for clarity.

Deity

A god, goddess, or spiritual entity invoked during spellwork or rituals for guidance, protection, or support. Different deities are associated with specific energies or aspects of life, such as love, wisdom, war, or the natural world.

Divination

The practice of seeking knowledge or guidance from spiritual sources, often through tools like tarot cards, runes, scrying mirrors, or pendulums. Divination helps provide insight into situations, decisions, and potential outcomes.

Elemental Magic

Magic that calls upon the natural elements—Earth, Air, Fire, Water, and sometimes Spirit—to aid in spellwork. Each element has its own properties and correspondences; for example, Earth is linked to stability and grounding, while Fire represents transformation and passion.

Energy

The life force or power that is directed during spellwork to bring about change. Energy can be drawn from the practitioner, natural elements, celestial bodies, or spiritual entities, and is often focused and shaped using magical tools, rituals, or intention.

Full Moon

A phase of the moon when it appears fully illuminated from Earth. The full moon is considered a powerful time for spells related to completion, manifestation, and amplifying intentions.

Grimoire

A personal book of spells, rituals, and magical knowledge kept by a practitioner. It serves as a record of magical work and often includes correspondences, incantations, and notes on spiritual experiences.

Grounding

A practice to connect oneself with the Earth's energy, helping to balance, calm, and stabilize the practitioner's own energy. Grounding techniques include visualizing roots growing from the body into the Earth, walking barefoot on soil, or holding grounding stones like hematite.

Herbs

Plants and plant materials used in spellwork for their magical properties. Each herb has specific correspondences; for example, rosemary is associated with purification and protection, while lavender promotes peace and relaxation.

Incantation

A spoken or chanted phrase used during spellwork to direct energy and focus intention. Incantations often rhyme or follow a rhythmic pattern to enhance their power.

Intent

The desired outcome or goal of a spell or ritual. Intent is the driving force behind spellwork, and clear, focused intent is essential for successful magic.

Knot Magic

A form of spellwork that involves tying knots in a cord or ribbon to bind or release energy. Each knot is tied with intention, representing aspects of the spell such as wishes, protection, or binding.

Moon Phases

The different phases of the moon, which influence the timing and focus of spells. New moon spells are ideal for new beginnings, while waning moon spells are suited for banishing and letting go.

Pentacle

A symbol of a five-pointed star enclosed within a circle, representing the elements and spirit. It is often used in spellwork for protection and balance.

Potion

A liquid mixture of herbs, oils, and other magical ingredients used in spells and rituals. Potions can be consumed, anointed on objects, or sprinkled around spaces for their intended effect.

Protection

Spells and rituals designed to shield the practitioner, their home, or loved ones from negative energies, entities, or influences. Protection spells often involve herbs like sage, salt, crystals, or protective symbols.

Purification

The process of cleansing a person, object, or space of negative energies. Purification can be achieved through smudging, saltwater baths, candle burning, or visualization techniques.

Ritual

A ceremonial act performed with intention to create a specific change or to honor spiritual practices. Rituals can involve various elements such as candles, incense, crystals, and incantations.

Samhain

An ancient Celtic festival celebrated on October 31st, marking the end of the harvest season and the beginning of the darker half of the year. Samhain is a time when the veil between the physical and spiritual worlds is believed to be thinnest, making it a powerful occasion for divination, honoring ancestors, and spellwork.

Scrying

A form of divination that involves gazing into a reflective surface, such as a mirror, crystal ball, or water, to receive visions or insights from the subconscious or spiritual realm.

Sigil

A symbol created and charged with intent for use in spellwork. Sigils are often drawn, carved, or burned onto objects to invoke specific energies or intentions.

Smudging

The act of burning herbs, typically sage, to cleanse a space, object, or person of negative energies. The smoke is believed to purify and raise the vibrational energy of the environment.

Spell

A focused and intentional act of directing energy to manifest a desired outcome. Spells often involve rituals, incantations, symbols, and correspondences to align the practitioner's intention with universal forces.

Talisman

An object that is charged with magical energy to bring about a specific effect, such as protection, luck, or love. Talismans can be worn, carried, or placed in a significant location.

Visualization

A mental practice where the practitioner imagines the desired outcome of a spell as if it is already happening. Visualization helps to focus energy and strengthen the intent behind the spell.

Waning Moon

The period when the moon's visible light decreases after a full moon. It is a time suitable for spells of banishing, releasing, and letting go of things that no longer serve you.

Waxing Moon

The phase of the moon between the new moon and the full moon, when the visible light increases. This period is ideal for spells related to growth, attraction, and building new habits.

Wicca

A modern pagan religion that emphasizes nature worship, the elements, and the balance between the divine masculine and feminine. Wiccans often practice magic, celebrate seasonal festivals, and work with the phases of the moon.

Witchcraft

A broad term that refers to the practice of magic, spellwork, and rituals to influence reality. Witchcraft encompasses a variety of traditions, beliefs, and practices and is not limited to any single religion or spiritual path.

This glossary serves as a helpful reference for understanding the key terms and concepts involved in spellcasting, rituals, and magical practice. By familiarizing yourself with these definitions, you'll deepen your knowledge and confidence as you explore the magical arts.

Appendix B: Samhain Herbs and Ingredients Guide: Properties and Uses of Herbs, Plants, and Ingredients in Samhain Spells

Samhain is a powerful time for magic, divination, and honoring ancestors. The herbs, plants, and other ingredients used during this season carry deep symbolic meanings and magical properties. This guide provides an extensive look at the most common herbs and ingredients associated with Samhain, detailing their properties, uses, and the specific ways they can enhance spellwork during this sacred time. Understanding these natural components allows you to harness their energies effectively for your rituals, spells, and celebrations.

1. Apple

- **Properties:** Love, healing, divination, wisdom.
- **Uses:** Apples are traditionally associated with Samhain as they symbolize knowledge and the otherworld. They can be used in spells for love, divination, and connection to the spirit realm. Apple slices can be left as offerings to ancestors or spirits, while apple seeds can be used in spells for planting new intentions.
- **How to Use:** Incorporate apple slices into divination rituals or use apple cider in offerings. Peel an apple in one continuous strip for a fortune-telling ritual, asking a question and allowing the peel to form a shape that reveals the answer.

2. Bay Leaf

- **Properties:** Protection, wishes, strength, purification.
- **Uses:** Bay leaves are excellent for spells involving protection, banishing negativity, and manifesting wishes. During Samhain, they can be burned to ward off negative energies and create a protective boundary between the physical and spiritual realms.

- **How to Use:** Write a wish or intention on a bay leaf and burn it in a Samhain fire to release it to the universe. You can also place bay leaves under your pillow to enhance prophetic dreams during the thinning of the veil.

3. Cinnamon

- **Properties:** Protection, prosperity, passion, healing.
- **Uses:** Cinnamon is a warming spice that amplifies energy and intention. It's perfect for adding a boost to spells for protection, success, and personal power during Samhain. It also invites warmth and abundance into your life as the darker half of the year begins.
- **How to Use:** Sprinkle cinnamon in a ritual bath to attract prosperity or use it in candle magic by anointing a candle with cinnamon oil before burning it for enhanced spell potency.

4. Clove

- **Properties:** Protection, purification, banishing negativity, love.
- **Uses:** Cloves are known for their protective and purifying qualities, making them ideal for clearing away negative energies at Samhain. They can also be used in spells for attracting love and friendship.
- **How to Use:** Place cloves in a small sachet to carry for protection or add them to incense blends to purify your space. You can also add cloves to a simmering pot of water with other herbs to create a cleansing, protective aroma in your home.

5. Mugwort

- **Properties:** Psychic abilities, divination, dreams, protection.
- **Uses:** Mugwort is a classic herb for enhancing psychic abilities and dream work, particularly during Samhain when the veil between the worlds is thin. It is commonly used for scrying, clairvoyance, and connecting with spirits.

- **How to Use:** Burn dried mugwort as an incense to cleanse and prepare your space for divination. Place a small sachet of mugwort under your pillow to enhance prophetic dreams or create a tea (with caution) to open your psychic senses.

6. Rosemary

- **Properties:** Purification, protection, memory, love.
- **Uses:** Rosemary is an all-purpose herb with strong protective and purifying qualities. It is especially useful during Samhain for clearing away negative energies, enhancing memory (for ancestor work), and ensuring a safe space for spiritual activities.
- **How to Use:** Burn rosemary as a smudge to purify your home or add it to your ritual bath for cleansing. You can also use it to make a wreath or garland to hang over doorways for protection during the Samhain season.

7. Sage

- **Properties:** Purification, wisdom, protection, clarity.
- **Uses:** Sage is a powerful cleansing herb, often used to clear away negative energies and create a sacred space. During Samhain, sage helps protect and purify your environment, making it a safe space for divination and spirit communication.
- **How to Use:** Burn sage to cleanse your ritual space or carry a small bundle with you for personal protection. You can also use sage in anointing oils to enhance spiritual clarity.

8. Cinnamon Sticks

- **Properties:** Success, spiritual healing, love, protection.
- **Uses:** Cinnamon sticks are often used to stir potions and spell mixtures to infuse them with protective and success-enhancing properties. They can be added to spell jars, sachets, or used in prosperity and protection rituals during Samhain.

- **How to Use:** Use cinnamon sticks to stir your morning tea or coffee while focusing on your intention for the day. Add them to sachets for protection or to invoke warmth and abundance in your life.

9. Ginger

- **Properties:** Power, protection, love, success.
- **Uses:** Ginger is a fiery herb that adds power and speed to any spell or ritual. It can be used in Samhain spells to break through barriers, bring quick results, or add energy to protection rituals.
- **How to Use:** Add dried ginger to incense blends for an extra boost of energy. Use fresh ginger slices in ritual baths to invigorate your spirit and prepare for new beginnings.

10. Pumpkin

- **Properties:** Fertility, prosperity, protection, growth.
- **Uses:** Pumpkins are synonymous with Samhain and symbolize the harvest and abundance. Their seeds can be used in spells for prosperity, growth, and new beginnings, while the carved pumpkin itself serves as a protective lantern.
- **How to Use:** Carve a pumpkin into a jack-o'-lantern to protect your home from negative energies and spirits. Use the seeds in planting spells to set intentions for future prosperity.

11. Rosemary Oil

- **Properties:** Protection, purification, clarity, memory.
- **Uses:** Rosemary oil is highly versatile, adding its protective and purifying properties to anointing rituals. It is excellent for enhancing mental clarity, aiding in memory work (especially when honoring ancestors), and providing protection during Samhain spells.

- **How to Use:** Anoint candles, your third eye, or magical tools with rosemary oil to purify and enhance their power. Mix a few drops into your ritual bath to cleanse your aura and invite protection.

12. Sea Salt

- **Properties:** Purification, protection, grounding.
- **Uses:** Sea salt is a staple in magical practices, known for its ability to cleanse, purify, and protect. It is particularly useful during Samhain for creating protective circles, grounding energy, and banishing negativity.
- **How to Use:** Sprinkle sea salt in a circle around your ritual space for protection or dissolve it in a bath to cleanse and purify your body and spirit.

13. Frankincense

- **Properties:** Spirituality, purification, protection, healing.
- **Uses:** Frankincense is used in rituals to elevate spiritual energy, purify spaces, and connect with higher realms. During Samhain, it can help create a sacred environment for divination, spellwork, and communication with the spirit world.
- **How to Use:** Burn frankincense resin as an offering to ancestors or to cleanse your home. Add it to incense blends to enhance spiritual awareness and create a serene atmosphere for meditation.

14. Lavender

- **Properties:** Peace, healing, love, purification.
- **Uses:** Lavender is well-known for its calming and protective qualities. During Samhain, it can be used to create a peaceful atmosphere for rituals, promote restful sleep, and provide spiritual protection during dream work.

- **How to Use:** Add dried lavender to sachets for peace and protection or scatter it around your home to cleanse the space. Incorporate lavender into a dream pillow to enhance prophetic dreams.

15. Black Salt

- **Properties:** Protection, banishing, warding off negativity.
- **Uses:** Black salt is used to absorb and banish negative energies. It is especially powerful during Samhain for protecting against malevolent spirits and clearing out old, stagnant energy to make way for new beginnings.
- **How to Use:** Sprinkle black salt at doorways, windowsills, and around your property to ward off negative influences. Use it in banishing spells to remove obstacles from your path.

16. Rosemary

- **Properties:** Memory, purification, protection, healing.
- **Uses:** Rosemary is often used to honor ancestors, clear negative energies, and provide protection. During Samhain, it aids in connecting with the past, recalling memories, and setting intentions for the future.
- **How to Use:** Burn rosemary to purify your space or place sprigs on your altar to honor your ancestors. Add rosemary to a ritual bath to cleanse your aura before spellwork.

17. Clove Oil

- **Properties:** Protection, prosperity, courage.
- **Uses:** Clove oil is potent for protection and courage, helping to fortify one's spirit when exploring new beginnings or engaging with the spirit realm during Samhain.
- **How to Use:** Anoint candles, doorways, or yourself with clove oil to invite protection and courage. Add a few drops to a bath to promote spiritual strength and resilience.

18. Wormwood

- **Properties:** Spirit communication, psychic powers, protection.
- **Uses:** Wormwood is a powerful herb for enhancing psychic abilities and facilitating communication with spirits, making it highly relevant for Samhain rituals. It also offers protective qualities to safeguard against unwanted energies during divination.
- **How to Use:** Burn wormwood as an incense during scrying or tarot reading sessions to enhance psychic clarity. Use caution, as wormwood can be potent and should not be ingested.

19. Yarrow

- **Properties:** Courage, love, psychic abilities, protection.
- **Uses:** Yarrow is a versatile herb that provides courage and protection. It is often used during Samhain to enhance psychic abilities, foster love, and create a shield of protection during spirit work.
- **How to Use:** Add yarrow to a sachet or mojo bag for protection and courage. Use yarrow tea (with caution) to boost psychic sensitivity during Samhain.

20. Orange Peel

- **Properties:** Joy, love, success, divination.
- **Uses:** Orange peel carries the vibrant energy of the sun, making it perfect for invoking joy, warmth, and success in your life as you set new intentions during Samhain. It also aids in divination practices.
- **How to Use:** Add dried orange peel to incense blends for success spells or sprinkle around your altar to attract positivity and joy.

This guide to Samhain herbs and ingredients serves as a valuable resource for spellcasters seeking to harness the natural magic of the season. By understanding the properties and uses of these elements, you can create more effective and meaningful rituals that align with your intentions during this mystical time of transformation and new beginnings. Use these herbs thoughtfully, honoring their energies as you work toward manifesting your desires and connecting with the spiritual realm.

Appendix C: Tools of the Trade: Overview of Spellcasting Tools

Spellcasting tools are fundamental to magical practice, helping practitioners focus their intent, direct energy, and create sacred spaces for rituals. Each tool carries its own symbolic meaning and serves specific purposes in spellwork. This appendix provides an in-depth overview of common spellcasting tools, detailing their functions, uses, and the ways they enhance magical practices. From wands to candles, understanding these tools is crucial for any practitioner looking to deepen their craft and make their rituals more powerful and effective.

1. Altar

- **Overview:** An altar is a sacred space or surface used as a focal point for magical work, rituals, and offerings. It serves as the central hub for spellcasting, housing tools, ingredients, candles, symbols, and representations of deities or spirits.
- **Use:** An altar can be set up anywhere, indoors or outdoors, depending on the practitioner's preference. Items on the altar often correspond to the four elements (Earth, Air, Fire, and Water) to create a balanced magical environment. For Samhain, an altar might include symbols of harvest, ancestors, protective herbs, and a candle to represent the thinning veil between worlds.
- **How to Use:** Arrange items that resonate with your spell's purpose on the altar. Cleanse the space before use to create a sacred, energetic atmosphere.

2. Wand

- **Overview:** A wand is a tool used to direct energy during spellwork and rituals. Typically made of wood, wands can be simple or intricately carved, sometimes adorned with crystals, feathers, or symbols to enhance their power.
- **Use:** Wands are ideal for casting circles, drawing symbols, and focusing energy. Different types of wood correspond to various magical purposes; for example, oak wands represent strength and wisdom, while willow wands are associated with intuition and healing.

- **How to Use:** Hold the wand in your dominant hand to direct energy. When casting a circle, point the wand toward the ground and envision a protective boundary forming. When working on specific spells, use the wand to channel your intent toward the desired outcome.

3. Athame

- **Overview:** The athame is a ritual knife, usually double-edged, symbolizing the element of Air (or Fire, in some traditions). It is not used for physical cutting but rather for directing energy, carving symbols, or cutting through spiritual barriers.
- **Use:** The athame is primarily used for casting circles, directing energy, and invoking elements during spellwork. It is a powerful tool for banishing negative energies, releasing unwanted attachments, and severing ties.
- **How to Use:** Hold the athame while visualizing your intent. Use it to draw symbols in the air, carve magical symbols into candles, or direct energy during spellcasting. For Samhain, the athame can be used in cord-cutting rituals to release old habits and attachments.

4. Cauldron

- **Overview:** The cauldron is a symbol of transformation, rebirth, and the womb of creation. Traditionally made of cast iron, cauldrons are used for mixing ingredients, burning herbs, creating potions, or as a vessel for scrying.
- **Use:** During Samhain, the cauldron is particularly significant as it represents the cycle of death and rebirth. It can be used for burning spells (such as releasing habits written on paper), brewing herbal potions, or creating protective smudge blends.
- **How to Use:** Place ingredients inside the cauldron for spellwork or light a candle within it to represent the inner flame of transformation. For scrying, fill the cauldron with water and gaze into its surface to receive insights and visions.

5. Chalice

- **Overview:** The chalice, often representing the element of Water, is a cup or goblet used in rituals to hold liquids such as water, wine, or herbal infusions. It symbolizes the divine feminine and is associated with intuition, emotions, and the subconscious.
- **Use:** The chalice is used in rituals for offerings, libations, or to symbolize the flow of energy. During Samhain, it can be filled with apple cider, wine, or water as an offering to ancestors and spirits.
- **How to Use:** Hold the chalice during rituals, focusing on its symbolism. Use it to make offerings by pouring a bit of liquid onto the ground or into a bowl as a gesture of respect to deities or spirits.

6. Candles

- **Overview:** Candles are essential tools in spellcasting, representing the element of Fire. Each candle's color corresponds to different energies and intentions: white for purity, black for protection and banishing, green for growth, red for passion, and so on.
- **Use:** Candles are used to focus intent, represent spiritual light, and act as a beacon for energy during rituals. In Samhain spellwork, black candles can be used to honor the dead and banish negativity, while orange candles can represent the harvest and the thinning veil.
- **How to Use:** Anoint candles with oils and carve symbols or runes into the wax before lighting them. When lighting a candle, speak your intention aloud and visualize its flame drawing your desires into reality.

7. Pentacle

- **Overview:** A pentacle is a five-pointed star enclosed in a circle, representing the balance of the elements (Earth, Air, Fire, Water) and Spirit. It often appears on altar cloths, jewelry, and other magical tools as a symbol of protection and unity.
- **Use:** The pentacle is used for grounding energy, protecting the space, and invoking elemental powers during rituals. It serves as a focal point for energy and can be placed on an altar to charge other tools and ingredients.
- **How to Use:** Place the pentacle on your altar as a symbol of unity and protection. During Samhain, it can serve as the central point of your spellwork, helping to balance and direct the energy you raise.

8. Incense Burner

- **Overview:** An incense burner is used to hold and burn incense, which is a blend of herbs, resins, and oils chosen for their aromatic and magical properties. Incense represents the element of Air and is used for purification, creating a sacred space, and enhancing psychic abilities.
- **Use:** During Samhain, incense burners can be used to burn scents associated with the season, such as sage for cleansing, mugwort for divination, or cinnamon for protection. The smoke from the incense carries intentions to the spiritual realm and creates an atmosphere conducive to ritual work.
- **How to Use:** Place loose herbs or incense cones in the burner, light them, and allow the smoke to fill the space. Pass your tools, candles, or crystals through the smoke to purify them before use in spellwork.

9. Bell

- **Overview:** A bell is a tool used to cleanse space, raise energy, and signal transitions in rituals. The ringing of a bell symbolizes the clearing of old energy and the invitation of new vibrations.
- **Use:** Bells can be rung to begin and end rituals, mark the casting and closing of a circle, or call upon spirits and deities. During Samhain, ringing a bell can help to clear the air, ward off negativity, and honor the presence of ancestral spirits.
- **How to Use:** Ring the bell while walking clockwise around your sacred space to clear negative energy. Use it at the start and end of your ritual to signify the opening and closing of the magical work.

10. Crystals

- **Overview:** Crystals are natural stones that hold various energetic properties. They are used to amplify intentions, protect spaces, enhance psychic abilities, and align the practitioner's energy with the desired outcome.
- **Use:** Each crystal has specific properties; for instance, amethyst enhances psychic awareness, rose quartz promotes love, and black tourmaline offers protection. During Samhain, crystals can be placed on the altar to honor ancestors, focus intentions, or ground energy.
- **How to Use:** Cleanse crystals by passing them through incense smoke or moonlight before use. Hold a crystal in your hand to charge it with your intention, then place it on your altar or carry it as a talisman during rituals.

11. Mortar and Pestle

- **Overview:** A mortar and pestle are used to grind herbs, spices, and resins into fine powders for spellwork. This tool represents the combination of the elements (herbs) with the practitioner's energy (grinding) to create potent magical ingredients.
- **Use:** During Samhain, use the mortar and pestle to prepare herbs for incense blends, sachets, potions, or candle dressing. The act of grinding releases the natural energies of the ingredients, making them more powerful in your spellwork.
- **How to Use:** Place the herbs or ingredients in the mortar and use the pestle to grind them while focusing on your intention. Visualize the energy of the herbs being activated and blending together to serve your spell's purpose.

12. Grimoire (Book of Shadows)

- **Overview:** A grimoire, also known as a Book of Shadows, is a personal journal used to record spells, rituals, magical correspondences, and spiritual experiences. It is an invaluable tool for documenting one's journey and refining spellcraft over time.
- **Use:** The grimoire is where practitioners keep detailed notes on their practices, including the outcomes of spells, dreams, meditations, and insights. During Samhain, it's common to review past entries and reflect on the growth that has occurred since the last cycle.
- **How to Use:** Write down the details of each spell or ritual you perform, including ingredients, intentions, and results. Use your grimoire as a reference guide and a way to track your progress in your magical practice.

13. Offering Bowl

- **Overview:** An offering bowl is a small dish or vessel used to hold offerings to deities, spirits, or ancestors. It represents gratitude, respect, and the practitioner's connection to the spiritual realm.
- **Use:** During Samhain, the offering bowl is often filled with items such as herbs, food, wine, or coins to honor ancestors and the spirits of the departed. Offerings can be left on the altar or placed outside as a sign of respect.
- **How to Use:** Place the offering in the bowl, focusing on the intention of gratitude or reverence. Speak words of thanks or prayer as you present the offering.

14. Salt

- **Overview:** Salt is a natural substance with strong purifying, protective, and grounding properties. It is used to cleanse spaces, protect against negative energies, and seal spells.
- **Use:** Sprinkle salt around your sacred space to create a protective boundary. Use it to purify tools before spellwork or add it to ritual baths for spiritual cleansing. During Samhain, salt can be used to protect your home from unwanted spirits or energies.
- **How to Use:** To cast a protective circle, sprinkle salt clockwise around the area where you will perform your spell. Dissolve salt in water for anointing or cleansing tools.

This appendix provides a comprehensive look at the primary tools used in spellcasting. By understanding each tool's purpose and how to use it effectively, practitioners can enhance their rituals and spellwork, making their magical practices more potent and focused. Whether you're preparing for a Samhain ceremony or any other magical work, these tools form the foundation of a successful and meaningful practice.

Appendix D: Additional Resources: Suggested Readings, Websites, and Communities for Further Exploration of Samhain Spellcraft

Samhain is a deeply magical time that offers rich opportunities for spellcasting, divination, and spiritual growth. This appendix provides an extensive list of additional resources, including books, websites, online communities, and other materials to help you deepen your understanding of Samhain spellcraft. These resources cover a wide range of topics such as witchcraft, herbalism, rituals, divination, and folklore, allowing you to explore various aspects of Samhain and magical practices in greater depth.

Whether you are a novice or a seasoned practitioner, these recommended resources will enhance your knowledge and guide your journey into the mystical and transformative energies of Samhain.

1. Suggested Readings

The following books are excellent starting points for those looking to explore Samhain, spellcraft, witchcraft, and related practices. These texts range from beginner-friendly guides to advanced explorations of magic, ritual, and the spiritual significance of Samhain.

Books on Samhain and Sabbats

- **"Samhain: Rituals, Recipes & Lore for Halloween" by Diana Rajchel**
  - **Overview:** This comprehensive book delves into the traditions, history, and rituals of Samhain. It includes practical tips for modern witches on how to celebrate and utilize the energy of Samhain in spellcraft and rituals.
  - **Why Read:** Perfect for those seeking an in-depth understanding of Samhain's magical significance, along with spells, recipes, and activities tailored to the season.
- **"The Witches' Wheel of the Year: Rituals for Circles, Solitaries & Covens" by Jason Mankey**
  - **Overview:** This book covers the eight sabbats of the Wiccan Wheel of the Year, including Samhain. It offers detailed information on how to celebrate and honor the cycles of nature through rituals, meditations, and spellcraft.
  - **Why Read:** An essential guide for practitioners wanting to integrate Samhain into a larger practice of seasonal celebrations.

- **"Llewellyn's Sabbats Almanac: Samhain 2024 to Mabon 2025" by Llewellyn**
    - **Overview:** This almanac provides seasonal insights, rituals, recipes, and articles related to each of the Wiccan sabbats. The Samhain section is particularly rich in lore, spells, and traditions.
    - **Why Read:** Ideal for those seeking year-round guidance for celebrating each sabbat, with a special focus on practical applications during Samhain.

Books on Witchcraft and Spellcasting

- **"The Modern Witchcraft Spell Book: Your Complete Guide to Crafting and Casting Spells" by Skye Alexander**
    - **Overview:** A comprehensive guide to spellcraft that covers a variety of magical practices, tools, and techniques. It includes detailed explanations of how to create and cast spells, making it accessible for both beginners and experienced witches.
    - **Why Read:** Provides a solid foundation for understanding the mechanics of spellcraft, which can be adapted and tailored for Samhain rituals and spells.
- **"Wicca Book of Spells: A Book of Shadows for Wiccans, Witches, and Other Practitioners of Magic" by Lisa Chamberlain**
    - **Overview:** This book offers an introduction to Wiccan spellcraft, with a focus on simple, practical spells for various intentions. It includes a section on seasonal magic that can be adapted for Samhain.
    - **Why Read:** A user-friendly guide for those interested in Wiccan spellcasting, offering insight into crafting spells that align with the energies of Samhain.

Books on Herbalism and Magical Ingredients

- **"The Complete Book of Incense, Oils & Brews" by Scott Cunningham**
    - **Overview:** This classic work provides recipes and instructions for creating magical incense, oils, brews, and other spellcraft supplies. It includes correspondences and properties of various herbs and plants.

- ◦ **Why Read:** A valuable resource for crafting your own herbal blends, incenses, and oils tailored to Samhain spellwork.
- **"Encyclopedia of Magical Herbs" by Scott Cunningham**
    - ◦ **Overview:** A detailed reference guide to over 400 herbs and their magical properties, this book includes uses, correspondences, and how to incorporate herbs into spells and rituals.
    - ◦ **Why Read:** Essential for those who wish to deepen their knowledge of herbal magic, particularly for creating herb-based Samhain spells.

Books on Divination and Psychic Abilities

- **"The Psychic Witch: A Metaphysical Guide to Meditation, Magick & Manifestation" by Mat Auryn**
    - ◦ **Overview:** This book explores the development of psychic abilities and their use in magical practices, providing exercises and techniques to enhance intuition, energy work, and spellcraft.
    - ◦ **Why Read:** Perfect for those who want to focus on psychic development and divination during the spiritually charged period of Samhain.
- **"Tarot for Beginners: A Practical Guide to Reading the Cards" by Lisa Chamberlain**
    - ◦ **Overview:** A practical guide to understanding and using tarot for divination, this book covers card meanings, spreads, and tips for intuitive readings.
    - ◦ **Why Read:** Ideal for those seeking to integrate tarot into their Samhain rituals and spells for deeper insight and guidance.

2. Online Resources and Websites

The internet is a vast source of information for modern practitioners. The following websites offer articles, forums, and guides on a variety of topics related to Samhain, witchcraft, and spellcraft.

Samhain and Witchcraft Websites

- **Witchvox (www.witchvox.com)**
  - **Overview:** A longstanding community-driven site for witches and pagans, Witchvox offers articles on spellcraft, rituals, seasonal celebrations, and local events. It is a great resource for connecting with other practitioners.
  - **Why Visit:** Provides extensive information on Samhain practices, rituals, and community events.
- **Llewellyn Worldwide (www.llewellyn.com)**
  - **Overview:** Llewellyn's website offers articles, guides, and books on a wide range of topics including spellcraft, witchcraft, and seasonal magic. Their collection includes expert contributions from well-known authors in the field.
  - **Why Visit:** Find insightful articles on Samhain spellcraft, tools, and seasonal correspondences.
- **The Witch of Lupine Hollow (www.witchoflupinehollow.com)**
  - **Overview:** A blog dedicated to modern witchcraft, the site provides guides, courses, and rituals centered around seasonal celebrations, including Samhain.
  - **Why Visit:** Excellent for finding practical and creative ideas for celebrating Samhain and incorporating seasonal magic into daily life.

Herbal and Ingredient Guides

- **The Herbal Academy (www.herbalacademy.com)**
  - **Overview:** An educational website offering courses, articles, and guides on herbalism, including the use of herbs in magical practices.
  - **Why Visit:** Useful for learning about the properties of Samhain herbs and how to safely incorporate them into spells and rituals.
- **Cunningham's Encyclopedia of Magical Herbs (www.cunninghamsherbs.com)**
  - **Overview:** An online companion to the book, providing additional resources, recipes, and herb profiles.
  - **Why Visit:** Offers an in-depth look at herbs' magical properties, ideal for creating herbal blends for Samhain spells.

3. Online Communities and Forums

Engaging with online communities allows you to share knowledge, ask questions, and connect with like-minded practitioners. These platforms offer forums, discussion boards, and virtual spaces where you can explore Samhain spellcraft.

Witchcraft and Pagan Communities

- **Reddit – r/witchcraft (www.reddit.com/r/witchcraft)**
  - **Overview:** A vibrant online community where practitioners of all levels discuss topics related to witchcraft, spells, rituals, and seasonal celebrations.
  - **Why Join:** Engage in conversations, ask questions, and seek advice on Samhain practices, spellwork, and related topics.

The Witches' Circle on Facebook

- - **Overview:** A Facebook group dedicated to discussions about witchcraft, spellcasting, and seasonal rituals.
  - **Why Join:** A supportive community that offers tips, resources, and discussions focused on various aspects of magic, including Samhain.
- **Witchy Amino (Amino Apps)**
  - **Overview:** A mobile app-based community for witches, pagans, and spiritual practitioners. It features discussion boards, blogs, and chatrooms dedicated to a variety of topics.
  - **Why Join:** A great place to explore different perspectives on Samhain spellcraft and find inspiration for your own rituals and practices.

4. YouTube Channels and Podcasts

Watching or listening to experienced practitioners can provide visual and auditory learning opportunities. Many content creators focus on seasonal magic, rituals, and spellcraft related to Samhain.

YouTube Channels

- **Harmony Nice**
  - **Overview:** A popular witchcraft YouTuber who covers a wide range of topics, including sabbat celebrations, spellcraft, and beginner tips.
  - **Why Watch:** Find tutorials and discussions on creating Samhain rituals, setting up altars, and crafting spells.
- **The Witch of Wonderlust**
  - **Overview:** A channel that offers practical witchcraft tips, spellwork guides, and seasonal celebrations.
  - **Why Watch:** Provides informative and accessible content on celebrating Samhain and incorporating its energies into spellcraft.

Podcasts

- **"The Witch Wave" by Pam Grossman**
    - ◦ **Overview:** A podcast featuring interviews with modern witches, artists, and writers. It covers a wide range of topics, including seasonal magic and spiritual practices.
    - ◦ **Why Listen:** Offers insight into the practice of witchcraft and celebrates the mystical aspects of Samhain.
- **"The Magick and Alchemy Podcast" by Tamed Wild**
    - ◦ **Overview:** A podcast focusing on magical practices, rituals, and the Wheel of the Year, including episodes dedicated to Samhain.
    - ◦ **Why Listen:** Explore in-depth discussions about the energies of Samhain, magical correspondences, and spellcraft.

This appendix serves as a guide to further resources, providing pathways for deeper exploration and understanding of Samhain spellcraft. Whether you prefer books, websites, community discussions, or audiovisual content, these resources are curated to support and inspire your magical journey. Embrace the season of Samhain with confidence, knowing that there is a wealth of knowledge and support available to enhance your practice.

Message from the Author:

I hope you enjoyed this book, I love astrology and knew there was not a book such as this out on the shelf. I love metaphysical items as well. Please check out my other books:

-Life of Government Benefits

-My life of Hell

-My life with Hydrocephalus

-Red Sky

-World Domination:Woman's rule

-World Domination:Woman's Rule 2: The War

-Life and Banishment of Apophis: book 1

-The Kidney Friendly Diet

-The Ultimate Hemp Cookbook

-Creating a Dispensary(legally)

-Cleanliness throughout life: the importance of showering from childhood to adulthood.

-Strong Roots: The Risks of Overcoddling children

-Hemp Horoscopes: Cosmic Insights and Earthly Healing

- Celestial Hemp Navigating the Zodiac: Through the Green Cosmos

-Astrological Hemp: Aligning The Stars with Earth's Ancient Herb

-The Astrological Guide to Hemp: Stars, Signs, and Sacred Leaves

-Green Growth: Innovative Marketing Strategies for your Hemp Products and Dispensary

-Cosmic Cannabis

-Astrological Munchies

-Henry The Hemp

-Zodiacal Roots: The Astrological Soul Of Hemp

- **Green Constellations: Intersection of Hemp and Zodiac**

-Hemp in The Houses: An astrological Adventure Through The Cannabis Galaxy

-Galactic Ganja Guide

Heavenly Hemp

Zodiac Leaves

Doctor Who Astrology

Cannastrology

Stellar Satvias and Cosmic Indicas

<u>Celestial Cannabis: A Zodiac Journey</u>

AstroHerbology: The Sky and The Soil: Volume 1

AstroHerbology:Celestial Cannabis:Volume 2

Cosmic Cannabis Cultivation

The Starry Guide to Herbal Harmony: Volume 1

The Starry Guide to Herbal Harmony: Cannabis Universe: Volume 2

Yugioh Astrology: Astrological Guide to Deck, Duels and more

Nightmare Mansion: Echoes of The Abyss

Nightmare Mansion 2: Legacy of Shadows

Nightmare Mansion 3: Shadows of the Forgotten

Nightmare Mansion 4: Echoes of the Damned

The Life and Banishment of Apophis: Book 2

Nightmare Mansion: Halls of Despair

<u>Healing with Herb: Cannabis and Hydrocephalus</u>

<u>Planetary Pot: Aligning with Astrological Herbs: Volume 1</u>

Fast Track to Freedom: 30 Days to Financial Independence Using AI, Assets, and Agile Hustles

<u>Cosmic Hemp Pathways</u>

How to Become Financially Free in 30 Days: 10,000 Paths to Prosperity

Zodiacal Herbage: Astrological Insights: Volume 1

Nightmare Mansion: Whispers in the Walls

The Daleks Invade Atlantis

Henry the hemp and Hydrocephalus

10X The Kidney Friendly Diet

Cannabis Universe: Adult coloring book

Hemp Astrology: The Healing Power of the Stars
Zodiacal Herbage: Astrological Insights: Cannabis Universe: Volume 2
<u>**Planetary Pot: Aligning with Astrological Herbs: Cannabis Universes: Volume 2**</u>
Doctor Who Meets the Replicators and SG-1: The Ultimate Battle for Survival
Nightmare Mansion: Curse of the Blood Moon
<u>**The Celestial Stoner: A Guide to the Zodiac**</u>
Cosmic Pleasures: Sex Toy Astrology for Every Sign
Hydrocephalus Astrology: Navigating the Stars and Healing Waters
Lapis and the Mischievous Chocolate Bar

Celestial Positions: Sexual Astrology for Every Sign
Apophis's Shadow Work Journal: : A Journey of Self-Discovery and Healing
Kinky Cosmos: Sexual Kink Astrology for Every Sign
Digital Cosmos: The Astrological Digimon Compendium
Stellar Seeds: The Cosmic Guide to Growing with Astrology
Apophis's Daily Gratitude Journal

Cat Astrology: Feline Mysteries of the Cosmos
The Cosmic Kama Sutra: An Astrological Guide to Sexual Positions
Unleash Your Potential: A Guided Journal Powered by AI Insights
Whispers of the Enchanted Grove

Cosmic Pleasures: An Astrological Guide to Sexual Kinks
369, 12 Manifestation Journal
Whisper of the nocturne journal(blank journal for writing or drawing)
The Boogey Book
Locked In Reflection: A Chastity Journey Through Locktober
Generating Wealth Quickly:
How to Generate $100,000 in 24 Hours
Star Magic: Harness the Power of the Universe

The Flatulence Chronicles: A Fart Journal for Self-Discovery
The Doctor and The Death Moth
Seize the Day: A Personal Seizure Tracking Journal
The Ultimate Boogeyman Safari: A Journey into the Boogie World and Beyond

If you want solar for your home go here: https://www.harborsolar.live/apophisenterprises/

Get Some Tarot cards: https://www.makeplayingcards.com/sell/apophis-occult-shop

Get some shirts: https://www.bonfire.com/store/apophis-shirt-emporium/

Instagrams:
@apophis_enterprises,
@apophisbookemporium,
@apophisscardshop
Twitter: @apophisenterpr1 Tiktok:@apophisenterprise
Youtube: @sg1fan23477, @FiresideRetreatKingdom

Podcast: Apophis Chat Zone: https://open.spotify.com/show/5zXbr-CLEV2xzCp8ybrfHsk?si=fb4d4fdbdce44dec

Newsletter: https://apophiss-newsletter-27c897.beehiiv.com/